THE POLISH August

The events, which took place in Poland in August 1980, brought about a turning point in the history of post-war Europe. This breach in the unity of the Soviet bloc opened the way to the breakdown of a totalitarian system which had triumphed after the II World War. The history of those eighteen days from 14th to 31st August, encompasses – in a nutshell – the entire journey from enslavement to freedom of a society emerging from under the yoke of Communism.

Something took place in Poland, which nobody had planned or foreseen. The least that even the initiators of the strike in the Gdańsk Shipyard – members of an organised democratic Opposition – could hope for was one more small step towards freedom. The toast drunk by Russian dissidents "To the success of our hopeless task!" continued to ring true in all the countries of the Communist bloc.

However, even after only a few days of this strike, hopes rose to astonishing proportions. The gauntlet thrown by the Opposition drew a public response akin to that seen during the first pilgrimage of Pope John Paul II to his homeland in June 1979, when the Polish public suddenly realised that it had a power which was quite independent of the structures of the Communist state. A year later, people flocked to the Shipyard.

During those extraordinary days, the Opposition, previously scattered, often at loggerheads, now spoke with one voice. The strikers' motto, in the guise of The Twenty-One Demands, became a weapon against the authorities, a symbol which opened doors normally inaccessible to the Opposition. And Lech Wałęsa became their champion.

The totalitarian system, which just a moment previously had seemed so unshakeable, was now faced with denial. And, just as the Shipyard became an oasis of freedom reaching out to the whole nation, so Poland, too, would soon begin to influence Eastern Europe. Public solidarity became a force to be reckoned with. The Poles were the first to demonstrate that a united public stand against the Communist authorities could change the course of politics.

Polish society, which up to this moment had been split, suddenly took up a united stand for its rights. Seeing the scale of this challenge, those in authority were, for many months, reluctant to quell this mass movement. The Soviet Union decided against intervention by force...

Our story recounts, day by day, the events of that fateful August in 1980 – each of those days being a huge step towards freedom.

*

In the Soviet bloc, the end of the 80's and the beginning of the 90's confirmed the importance to the history of Europe of the events of that August. On the one hand, they weakened the aggressive nature of the Communist system; on the other – they awoke the imagination of the public and strengthened its resolve. And even though military might lay only on one side, this was – nonetheless – a confrontation of two powers. The longer armed intervention was delayed, the greater grew the strength of the unarmed masses.

Initially, the Soviet Union was prepared to quell this rebellion with military force. The armies of the Warsaw Pact were ready to intervene in the Shipyard on 29th August, and on 8th December throughout Poland. Realising, however, that this moment was not conducive to success, the decision to call off the operation was taken at the last minute. Later, the Soviets were to make many threats to use force and the Poles were afraid this would, indeed, happen. However, by autumn 1981, they had decided against military intervention.

At this time, Polish Communists could not have been aware that, on 10th December 1981, just three days before martial law was introduced, one of the Soviet Leaders had announced in the Kremlin: *"We do not intend to send the army into Poland. This is the right decision and we should abide by it. I do not know what will happen but, even if Poland is taken over by «Solidarity», then that will be the end of the matter. [...] We have our own country to worry about"*. By its very agreement to the existence of a "Solidarity" run Poland, the Soviet Union was beginning to lose its global imperial might.

I

By introducing martial law, the Polish functionaries of the Communist system made their attack on Polish society in the name of that empire. They lost. Although they managed to temporarily paralyse Poland, the subsequent years of martial law could not restore the effective power of the authorities. Memories of the 10-million strong "Solidarity" movement hampered any thoughts the authorities might have had of repressions; in Moscow these memories gave an undoubted impetus to the politics of "Perestroyka", which recognised that nations could no longer be ruled solely by terror tactics.

By the year 1988, the mere threat of strike action in Poland was sufficient for a political compromise to be found. The decisions taken during the Round Table talks in Warsaw in April 1989 sent a signal to the whole of Eastern Europe. Waves of rebellion in Hungary, the Democratic Republic of Germany, in Czechoslovakia and the Baltic Republics showed that the passing years had not managed to silence the spreading wave of peaceful disobedience of those August days.

The events of the People's Spring of 1989 showed little resemblance to the "period of negotiation" in Poland in 1988/89 – indeed, they were more like the avalanche which built-up throughout August 1980. In symbolic terms, the western part of the Soviet bloc took the path which led from the gate of the Gdańsk Shipyard to the Brandenburg Gate. The fall of the Berlin Wall was to be the culmination of a process which had been brewing for many years. It did not end there, however.

The Soviet system prevailed in various guises in the eastern part of the one-time empire. The wave of freedom found its way there, too, and gained momentum – even in Russia – yet never caused a tide. In Byelorussia, it is now merely a ripple. But nowhere has it subsided completely.

The victory of the Orange Revolution in the Ukraine – yet another instance of a peaceful, mass denial of the status quo – was proof that the desire for freedom cannot be quelled in any society.

And it all started with those 18 days which shook our world.

July 2005   *Zbigniew Gluza*

Photo: Zbigniew Trybek

In December 1970, the shipyard workers in the Coastal Provinces went on strike. The strike was caused by the economic situation. Strikers, thrown into desperation by the refusal of the authorities to talk with them, massed in the streets. The First Secretary of the Polish United Workers Party (PZPR) gave instructions for the use of arms. The result was a massacre. The army and the militia fired not only on the crowds, which were storming and setting fire to Party Committee offices, but also on casual passers-by, and even on workmen making their way to work. On 16th December, at Gate No. 2 in the Gdańsk Shipyard, the army opened fire on striking workers trying to leave the Shipyard. Many people were killed or wounded.

There was then a change in the ruling team. At first, the new First Secretary of the Central Committee of the Polish United Workers Party, Edward Gierek, had some degree of standing among the workers. In 1976, the government once again attempted to introduce unexpected price rises and then brutally put an end to the strikes of workers in Radom and in Ursus. This led to the formation of the first openly active democratic opposition group – the Workers' Defence Committee (KOR), followed soon by other opposition organisations. In Gdańsk, where the memory of December 70 was still very fresh, an illegal organisation called Free Coastal Trade Unions (WZZ) was formed in April 1978. The underground journal "Robotnik" ("The Worker") was distributed in factories and then from 1978 the organisation had its own journal "Robotnik Wybrzeża" ("The Coastal Provinces Worker"), which also found its way to the Gdańsk Shipyard.

In June 1979 Polish society felt a great sense of unity thanks to the visit of Pope John Paul II. Gierek's epoch was drawing to an end, the country was sinking ever deeper into economic chaos, problems with obtaining basic goods were increasing drastically.

An attempt to introduce "surreptitious" rises in the price of meat and meat products on 1st July 1980 led to a sudden wave of strikes in many towns in Poland. The authorities tried to react swiftly; in the majority of cases, withdrawal of the new prices and promises of marginal price increases were enough to calm the situation for the time being. Most notable was the general strike in Lublin, where the authorities held talks with strike committees and where, apart from giving way on pay demands, they guaranteed the strikers' safety and undertook to hold new elections to factory boards.

The success of the July strikes was a vital signal for the Coastal Provinces.

The strike in the Gdańsk Shipyard started on 14th August. Apart from the personal notes, documents and photographs taken from those days, we would ask you to picture the reality of everyday life: queues in shops, high-rise housing, Party meetings and manifestations, military manouevres – these all provided the back-drop to the events of August 80.

Katarzyna Madoń-Mitzner

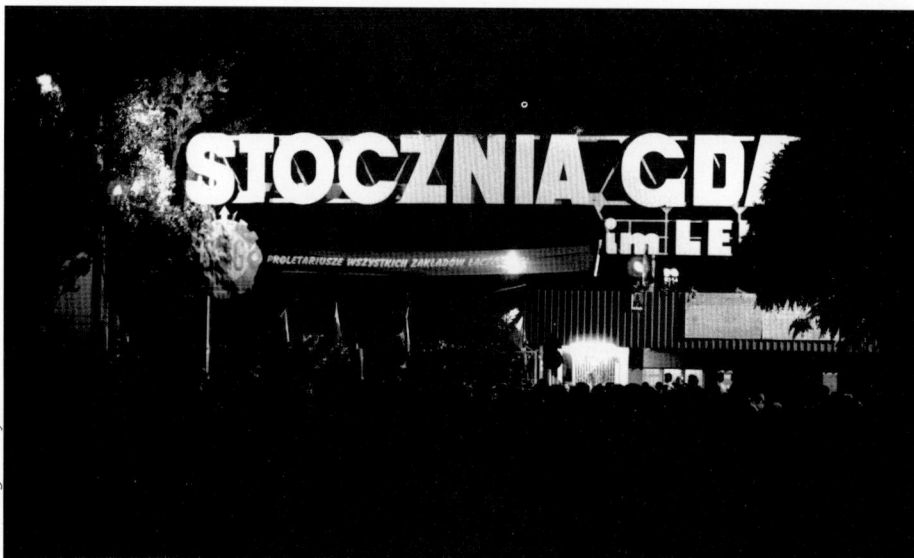

Prologue

Bogdan Borusewicz (KSS "KOR", WZZ):

From 1st August, I lived away from home and made preparations for the strike. Starting from technical matters, right up to the psychological attitudes of the initiating group. This was made up of three people from the Free Unions: Bogdan Felski, Ludwik Prądzyński and Jerzy Borowczak – all very young shipyard workers. [...] During one of the meetings [at the beginning of August], Prądzyński said: I heard on the ship that there was to be a strike, but there wasn't a strike. To which Felski said: that's right, that was me, I told them on

Bogdan Borusewicz

my ship that there was going to be a strike. [...] That meant there was an undercurrent, a strike mood.

[...] I wondered whether they would have the strength for such an undertaking. In the end I told them, and this was probably the deciding factor: *"I have no illusions that, following the sacking of Anna Walentynowicz, you are the next in line. By striking, you're saving your own skins, too"*.

[...] I had to organise the printing and write a leaflet. It was worded in such a way that, in the event of discovery during the printing process, it would not reveal vital information regarding the preparations for the strike. [...] I calculated that each shipyard worker should be handed a leaflet. In all, we printed some 12,000 copies. [...] I organised four groups of people who would distribute the leaflets on the suburban railways. [...]

On 10th August, in the apartment belonging to Piotr Dyka and his wife – quite close to the place where I was hiding out – Gdańsk opposition circles were celebrating the release of Dariusz Kobzdej and Tadeusz Szczudłowski [from the Movement for the Defence of Human and Civil Rights – ROPCiO], who had been arrested following the 3rd May demonstrations. So I called all three of them out to the courtyard, together with Wałęsa. It was then that Wałęsa learnt of the forthcoming strike and that it was also to include the Shipyard. Thus, the actual date of the strike was known to only five people – those who were to initiate it. [source: 26]

14-08-1980

Thursday

Edward Appel (Gdańsk):

Thursday 14th August did not herald anything particularly noteworthy – at least not as far as I was concerned. I had no hint of anything. Not even the small incident in the train, when a young man rushed through the carriage and pulled some leaflets out of his pocket, for which almost everybody made a grab, made any impression. I did not even try to get hold of one of the leaflets, I just wasn't interested, wasn't thinking. Anxiety about everyday realities, anxiety about "what to put in the saucepan" – that overshadowed everything else. [20]

Extract from leaflet:

Anna Walentynowicz became an embarrassment because her example motivated others. She became an embarrassment because she stood up for others and was able to organise her co-workers. The authorities always try to isolate those who have leadership qualities. If we do not fight against this, then we will have no-one who will stand up for us when they raise work quotas, when Health and Safety regulations are broken or when we are forced to work overtime. That is why we are appealing to you to come out in support of crane driver, Anna Walentynowicz. If you don't, many of you might find yourselves in the same situation.

Free Trade Unions Founding Committee and editorial staff of "Coastal Provinces Worker": Bogdan Borusewicz, Joanna Duda-Gwiazda, Andrzej Gwiazda, Jan Karandziej, Maryla Płońska, Alina Pienkowska, Lech Wałęsa

Jerzy Borowczak (Gdańsk Shipyard worker):

From the outset we knew that Lech would be in charge of the strike. People here knew him, knew him from all the anniversary celebrations and, after all, he had been elected to the Factory Board, and then thrown out. Everybody at the Shipyard knew Lech. We knew that he made good speeches, that he had a way with words, he'd made a speech at the December Anniversary here. The way he got them going – the crowd went wild! [34]

Bogdan Felski (Gdańsk Shipyard worker):

I went to one of the teams which I knew and began to explain to them what it is that we're fighting for. As I spoke, people began to get more daring. "Let's go", I said. And a group of 50 people got together. We made a banner for them. At that moment Barc, one of the managers, turned up and asked what was going on. "Mr Barc", I said "this is a strike". "A strike? What for? What's it about". So, I said: "Can't you read Mr Barc?" and showed him the banner. I also gave him several copies of "The Worker", and a statement concerning Anna [Walentynowicz] and then went off to get more people together. When I got back, Mazurkiewicz, the Departmental Secretary of Basal Party Organisation turned up and tried to take the banner away from us. The lads were quicker though and stopped him. The Secretary shouted: "What's going on?". They answered him: "Nothing that concerns you". Somebody managed to thrust some leaflets into his hand. They all surrounded him and began to laugh because it looked as if he was handing the leaflets out himself. However, I shouted: "Take them away from him" – I somehow didn't want the leaflets to find themselves in such undeserving hands. [7]

Emblem of Polish Resistance [lit: "Fighting Poland"] from the Second World War

The first strike poster, displayed on a digger

Jerzy Borowczak:

I arrived at the Shipyard at 4.15. When I had put up the posters, I got the leaflets ready – I had some 500 leaflets and I gave one to everybody who arrived at the Shipyard, saying: *"Here, take it and read! The whole Shipyard is on strike today!"*.

About 30 people got together and we marched off. Two colleagues carried a poster at the head. People were appearing everywhere to see what was going on. We shouted to them: *"Turn your machinery off and come and join us"*. Many did join us. So we made our way across the bridge, a larger crowd by now. People came out of the hulks. They said: *"We'll stop work but we can't come with you just yet"*. It was obvious they were afraid.

As I carried on through the Shipyard, I was quaking in my shoes. I wasn't afraid for myself but for those people who were following me. If they are sacked, they'll blame me, because I led them. And I kept saying: *"W-4 is at a standstill, K-3 isn't working. Come on, join us"*. But I wasn't to know. I thought to myself, if we get there and find people are working, the crowd is sure to go for me. That's what worried me. Here I am persuading people that all is well, I'm giving it my all and yet I don't believe it will work. [...]

We turned the corner and saw a group of people from K-3. We were at the third gate at the time, and they were some 500 metres further on. And then there was a roar *"Hurray"*. I knew then – we had a strike.

[...] We already had over a thousand people and it continued to grow – we couldn't see the end of the marching crowd. Every so often I would shin up a post to see the tail end. It was then we were sure that it would work. People came off the loaders, out of the hulks, went high

up onto the gantries, saw us and then came down. And, moment by moment, we could see that there were more of us. And dust – it was a sunny day – behind us there were clouds of dust.

We got up onto a digger, which was soon surrounded by a crowd of people. We made a speech: *"We must elect a strike committee. We need people we can trust, who have the confidence of the working teams. Come forward"*. Then the Director arrived with his entourage. We invited him up on the digger and helped him scramble up. As the Director began to speak, Lech Wałęsa suddenly arrived, came up behind him and said to him in a threatening voice: *"Do you recognise me? I worked at the Shipyard for ten years and still consider myself a shipyard worker, because I have a vote of confidence among the crew. I've been without work for four years now"*. And then he said: *"We're setting up a sit-in strike"*.

We then demanded that the Director's car should bring Mrs Anna Walentynowicz to the Shipyard. The Director protested but we insisted and shortly the Director's car was sent to bring Anna. We, ourselves, went on to the radio-station. And that is how the strike started. [7, 34]

Lech Wałęsa:

I travelled to the strike by tram. [...] I had heard the sirens at home and knew that it had already started. I couldn't leave any earlier because the housework had to be done. For the first few days after giving birth, Danuta was not very strong and this sixth child of ours – a little girl – was a handful.

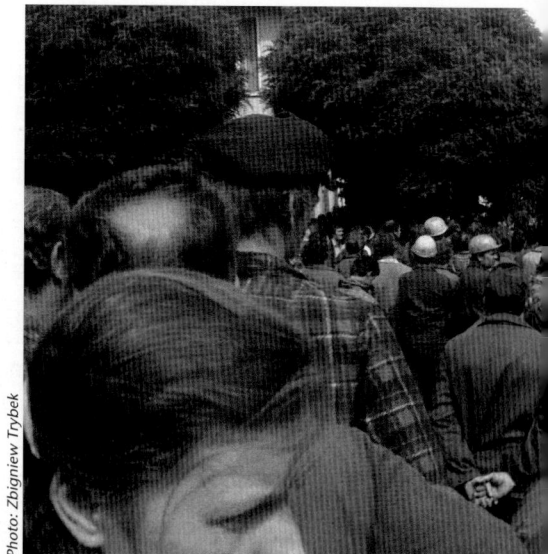

[...] People were massing by the second gate but the security men were checking passes carefully and I had not been allowed entry to the Shipyard for many years. I turned right, in the direction of the first gate and there, between the two gates, near the school, there's this little side street – I went there and jumped over the gate.

[...] You can have huge plans, ready scenarios, but people are only human – particularly when you stand on an earth mover, behind the back of the Director of the Shipyard, into which you have just crept like a thief, not having been there for four years – it's like jumping head first into a great unknown... [23]

Photo: Witold Górka

Anna Walentynowicz sorrounded by strikers

Anna Walentynowicz:

I learned from Alinka Pienkowska at the clinic at 7 a.m., that the strike had started. [...] I rushed out to the gate and there I saw four familiar "shadows", as they were getting out of a car. I made for my home, the men following after me. Taking advantage of the crowd crossing the road, I took refuge at a friend's home. I observed through the window as two women joined the four men: six people to arrest me!

I realised that I had to get to the Shipyard. Otherwise the Director would again say: " There you are – you're striking on her behalf and she can't be bothered to turn up". And he could well disperse the crowds with threats of punishment or sacking. I did not know then that the Director's car had already been sent for me. [10]

Jerzy Borowczak:

There were seven demands then. First was assurance that we would not be penalised for the strike. Then there was equalisation of benefits with the Ministry of the Interior and the Polish Army. Reinstatement of Walentynowicz and Wałęsa. And the formation [in the Shipyard] of Free Trade Unions, erections of a monument and wage rises of 2 thousand zloties. The formation of free trade unions was our most important demand, after all, we knew that without these there would be nothing. [...] We went to the Director. The Director said: *"Please, gentlemen, take a seat"*. Still in our safety helmets and greasy overalls, we scrambled for the chairs and armchairs... [34]

Strikers in front of the Shipyard Management building

Photo: Zbigniew Trybek

From the second round of talks between the strikers and the Directors of the Lenin Shipyard:

Lech Wałęsa:

We would remind you that this is a sit-in strike. If these matters are not resolved by 4 p.m. then we will organise ourselves – that is, appoint duty guards, ensure provisions and perhaps sleeping arrangements, and inform workers' families of the situation. That is why we ask everyone to stay put; at 4 p.m. we will know for certain: either everything is settled and we go home, or we sit it out to the end.

[...]

We want to have trade unions of our choice. Suitable people who will well and truly work in our common interest and fight for us.   [9]

Alina Pienkowska (Gdańsk Shipyard):

I ran from one home in the neighbourhood to another, asking for food for the strikers. Almost everyone opened their fridges and gave everything in them without the slightest hesitation. Despite the fact that there were no well-off people living in the street, we quickly managed to collect several sacks of food. To us, this marked the first important show of support from the general public.   [19]

Photo: Janusz Uklejewski/ADM/PAP

8

From a meeting of the Politburo of the Central Committee of the Polish United Workers Party:

Comrade Stanisław Kania:

The situation is worsening and taking a dangerous direction. The current strikes in Warsaw (one bus depot, two tram depots and part of the Civic Taxi Company) and Łódź (small factories in the Łódź area are on strike) have been joined by Gdańsk.

[...] The ring-leaders are two members of KOR and the sacked Wałęsa, who has ties with Kuroń's group. Power has been temporarily turned off on the ships under construction. [...] Demands are escalating. The following steps have been taken:

[...]

– party meetings and meetings of activists have been organised,

– agreement has been given to undertake discussions and to consider demands – but on the strict understanding that there is calm in the country and in Gdańsk,

– the forces of the Civil Militia have been re-grouped and three army regiments put on alert.

The situation is difficult because we are dealing with a tense atmosphere, indeed even with signs of hatred of the authorities. When the party itself is not too sure of its ground, then even the weakest opponent is a threat.

Comrade Mieczysław Jagielski:

[...] We have to inform Comrade Gierek of the situation and persuade him that his swift return from holiday is required.

In our propaganda, which should be serious and cautious, we should present the situation in such a way as to stem any rumours.

A television broadcast will shortly be essential. Its contents should take into account current social trends.   [24]

Extract from telexed information from the Provincial Committee of the Polish United Workers Party in Bielsko-Biała:

Having received official directives, the political officers made their way to 60 of the largest factories in our province, where they had meetings with the factories' party activists and points of first contact. [...] The party activists, as well as the workforces, wanted accurate information on the situation throughout the country. On checking, it turned out that, so far, the only sources of information getting through to factories were delivery drivers and Radio Free Europe; this then, in view of the lack of real information concerning current events, allied with production problems and the economic situation, has caused an atmosphere of uncertainty and tension among the workforces.   [1]

Photo: Maciej Osiecki

Key members of the Government and of the Communist Party. Centre: Edward Gierek

Photo: Jacek Kucharczyk

Woman in Queue:

My daughter came in, looked in the pans. She shouted that she was hungry, that she wants meat for dinner – there was nothing I could say, where am I to get it from? I promised that the following day I would go to the store, stand in the queue, perhaps I might get something.

I went out at eight in the morning and I was already twentieth in the queue but the shop doesn't open till eleven o'clock. There's this discussion in the queue. Everybody has something to say. For example: there wouldn't be any problem with food, you know, but our grub goes straight to the Soviet Union [...]. Then there were arguments – mainly with the disabled – that they take their places at the head of the queue every day and then sell the meat. One disabled man pushes in front of another one and shouts that he is more deserving and that he should have priority. The other one answers him: get lost man, you probably lost that leg because you were drunk. Children are complaining to their mothers. I don't know what would have happened next but at that moment a woman standing in the ordinary queue fainted. There was a sudden silence in the shop, as though everyone felt ashamed.

At last I reached the counter and got a piece of shoulder, half a kilo of sausage – that was the norm. I returned home, it was about 1.30 p.m. I put the dinner on, at the same time I hoovered the flat, washed the breakfast dishes. I keep smoking one cigarette after another, I'm a bundle of nerves, I don't even want to eat anything when I think about having to stand there again for so long tomorrow. It's all too much for me. In the morning I'll have to go out and look for some sour cream and butter...

My son and daughter-in-law came to visit us today. He says that there are strikes in some of the towns. My husband said it was nonsense, that these were just rumours spread in the queues. But I have a feeling that it's true – sooner or later it must come to that.

[15]

Lenin Gdańsk Shipyard

II

15-08-1980

Friday

- *The strike spreads to other shipyards, ports and public transport in the Triple City of Gdańsk, Gdynia and Sopot.*
- *The authorities cut off telephone links between the Coastal Provinces and the rest of Poland.*
- *Edward Gierek, First Secretary of the Polish United Workers' Party, breaks off his holiday in the Crimea.*

Bronisław Petlic (worker, Gdynia):

On 15th August local community news carried the word "strike". I came home from my night shift and told my wife: something's about to happen, you'd better stock up with food.   [20]

Andrzej Kołodziej (Gdynia Shipyard worker):

I was going to the Shipyard by bus and everyone in the bus already knew about the strike in the Gdańsk Shipyard; so there was some discussion: what about us, should we go on strike, too? I interrupted, saying: "Why, don't you know? We're not working today either, everything is ready and we're starting our own strike".

"How do you know?"

"I went to the Gdańsk Shipyard today and spoke to people. I'm not starting work and nor should you. For the moment, until it's time to start work, nobody will be any the wiser, but then everyone will know."   [25]

Bernard Pogorzelski (Gdynia Shipyard worker):

Shipyard workers stood against the barriers on all levels of the stern, staring in the direction of Department W-2. To me, it looked as though they were sort of excited, talking among themselves. I thought to myself – an accident, or something – and so I switched off my tools and joined them. From there you could see crowds of shipyard workers marching from the direction of the pipe works towards the main gate. I realised that something very important must have happened; there were shouts – strike, strike. I suddenly had a funny feeling, a shiver went down my back.

In front of the gate there was an old derelict shipyard trolley, and on it a slim, shortish figure, dressed in shipyard overalls – it was

Andrzej Kołodziej (on the trolley) addresses the strikers. Shipyard in Gdynia

Andrzej [Kołodziej]. He kept repeating the same words: *"All shipyard workers are asked to go to the main gate"*. [20]

Józef Sędziak (Gdynia Shipyard worker):

Andrzej stood there all day on that trolley, without even a break for a meal, calmly explaining that we would win the strike, that we are not alone, that other factories and workplaces in the Triple City of Gdańsk, Gdynia and Sopot are on strike, too. He also called on the management to make known their stance in relation to the striking workforce. So we stood there until the evening and, I must confess, I had a sneaking hope that in the evening we would go home – but it was not to be, because at dusk Andrzej said we would not disperse and that everyone would spend the night in the forecourt by the gate, as the night promised to be warm. [20]

Lech Wałęsa (at the end of yet another round of talks between the strikers and the Gdańsk Shipyard Management):

Seeing that the matter has, after all, been thrown out – we are at a standstill. We will not go back. I propose that everyone – every department and every individual – should make early arrangements for food provisions and then be prepared to spend the night in the Shipyard. [...] By ourselves – even though there are some one hundred of us, or perhaps a little more – we will not be able to achieve everything we set out to win for you. So, I suggest you prepare for yet another night. [9]

Bernard Pogorzelski (Gdynia Shipyard):

At about midnight, at Andrzej's request, my two brothers and I reported for sentry duty at the gate, near the management offices. Bonfires were lit every 30–40 metres along a several hundred metre stretch of pavement around the perimeter. At each bonfire there were groups of several people. This was a very key point in the defence, seeing that a possible attack could be launched from the direction of Czechosłowacka Street.

The Port of Gdynia, which had also joined the strike, placed railway engines in its gates, the gaps along the sides being filled with barricades. [20]

> ### Extract from a Statement issued by Ruch Młodej Polski (Movement for Young Poland):
>
> The Communists have been ruling for 35 years. They usurped power without a mandate from Polish society and they never tried to obtain such a mandate. [...] They took all decisions - society was merely the object of their manipulations and experiments. It is they who must take the full blame for the current crisis,
>
> [...] The only way forward lies in careful organisation and sensible demands for our rights. We must not allow ourselves to be provoked nor to look for victory through the use of force.

> ### Extract from an article in "Trybuna Ludu" ("People's Tribune"):
>
> There is nothing so unsettling as the silence of a motionless factory, dead machines and instruments which stand useless, unused, silent. They cannot answer the call for our increasing needs. In such an atmosphere we will never be able to think anything through or to work anything out. [...] Responsibility: what meaning has that today? Can that concept have any relation to continued stand-stills?

> ### Extract from a note in the "Głos Wybrzeża" ("Coastal Provinces Voice"):
>
> Disruption of work gives rise to anxiety, since it serves only to worsen the already difficult economic situation, to reduce the amount of goods and services being produced, which we all need and which we search for in the shops.

Photo: Chris Niedenthal/FORUM

Extract from a meeting of the Politburo of the Central Committee of the Polish United Workers Party:

Comrade Edward Gierek:

Thank you to all those comrades who were available and who tried to contain the un-called for events. Those of you who were on so-called leave did not have it easy either. We were kept fully informed.

[...]

Comrade Stanisław Kania:

[...] Increasingly, this has all the marks of a general strike. Comrade Fiszbach rates the situation as being dangerous. In the Shipyard some say that they should take to the streets, but others oppose this view. Kuroń's crowd do not push for it. This group behaves differently to Moczulski's. However, there is no guarantee that it will not happen. [...]

Comrade Edward Gierek:

And where are the Party members?

Comrade Stanisław Kania:

They do not have the strength to take counter measures. There was no inkling that a strike was being prepared. They were caught unawares. Employees of the Central Committee, the Ministry of the Interior, the Ministry of Heavy and Agricultural Machinery were sent to Gdańsk. The danger of unrest is real. That is why a state of emergency has been put on alert and law and order forces and the army have been deployed near Gdańsk.

[24]

Extract from telexed information from the Provincial Committee in Olsztyn to the Central Committee of the Polish United Workers Party:

In work places and in the urban communities we have noted an uneasy atmosphere and social tension. [...] Apart from news brought in from various parts of the country, the current situation and public feeling is negatively influenced by the availability of goods and raw production materials, as well as the availability on the market of basic food products. Every day, starting early in the morning, long queues form outside butchers' shops and food-stores selling flour, sugar, and butter – malicious tongues liken these queues to the queues outside Lenin's mausoleum. [1]

Photo: Jacek Kucharczyk

Sign above door: Meat, Meat Products

Extract from telex information sent by the Deputy Manager of the Organisational Department of the Provincial Committee in Płock to the Central Committee of the Polish United Workers Party:

For several days now we have been seeing signs of activity aimed at increasing public anxiety in the environs of the town of Kutno. Instances have been noted of anonymous telephone calls, informing about the need to prepare for a general strike throughout the country. There have also been instances of telephone calls to, for instance, the PKO [National Savings Bank], saying that a bomb has been placed in the building. Jehovah's Witnesses have also recently become more active, making visits to private homes and foretelling the outbreak of a III World War. [...]

Food stores in most towns are experiencing long queues of people waiting from early morning for deliveries of sugar. It should be noted that queues waiting for sugar are longer than those at butchers' shops. In Gostynin there was an incident where a customer forced his way to the other side of the counter and broke the finger of the shop assistant who tried to prevent this form of shopping for sugar. [1]

16-08-1980

Saturday

- *The strike in the Gdańsk Shipyard transforms itself into a solidarity strike; during the night, representatives of 21 workplaces form an Inter-factory Strike Committee.*
- *The Ministry of the Interior sets up a headquarters group to direct operation "Summer 80".*
- *In the Central Committee of the Polish United Workers Party a team, headed by Stanisław Kania, is set up to "co-ordinate government activities in the liquidation of strikes".*

Edward Appel (economist, Gdańsk Shipyard):

It is almost 3 p.m. The speakers, which so far have remained silent, suddenly emit crackles, followed by knocks, over which can be heard the clamour of raised voices, and then Wałęsa's voice takes over: *"We have reached an agreement, we have signatures guaran-teeing that our demands will be met. I pronounce the Gdańsk Shipyard strike over..."*.

We congratulate and hug each other. We can't stop the tears.

Discussing the events of these last hours, we make our way in the direction of the third gate. We are near the gate and push our way into the billowing crowd which is trying to make its way out. It seems, however, that the gate is shut.

What's the matter? – the question comes from all round us. And then we hear – the Shipyard strike is, indeed, over but a solidarity strike has just begun. It transpires that delegates from other, smaller workplaces, which do not have the clout to ensure their own demands are met positively, have asked the Shipyard leaders for help. [20]

Bogdan Borusewicz:

When the final demand – for money – had been agreed, I told my colleagues that we had to ensure the safety of the strikers. To which the Director replied that he must first consult with Fiszbach [First Secretary of the Provincial Committee of the Polish United Workers Party in Gdańsk]. He went off and another two hours passed. Then he returned and said: *"That's settled, Fiszbach promised"*. One of the lads shouted that there should be an official signature from the Provincial governor, but there was already a mood of joy, of light-heartedness; Wałęsa had the microphone. The Director said: *"We are ending the strike"* and Lech replied: *"Yes, we're ending it"*. This was broadcast over the whole factory and the Director immediately shut down the broadcasting system. Everyone got up from the table and then Mrs Henryka Krzywonos

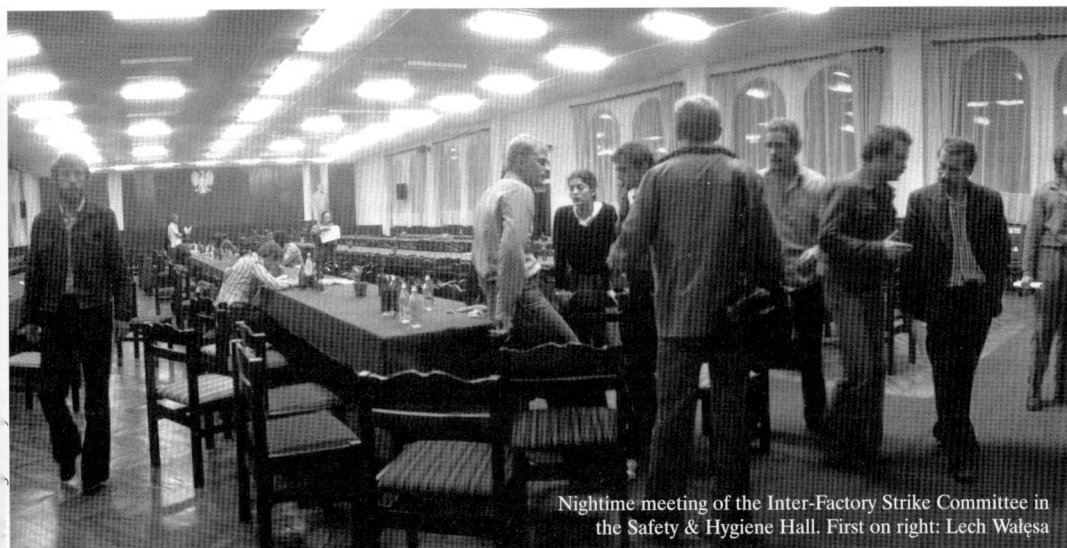

Nightime meeting of the Inter-Factory Strike Committee in the Safety & Hygiene Hall. First on right: Lech Wałęsa

from the Civic Transport Company (MPK) ran into the room and hurled herself at Lech shouting: *"You've sold us out! Now they'll crush all the small factories like insects underfoot"*. Wałęsa asked what could be done. I said that I didn't know, that it was over. I felt really helpless. Then Wałęsa grabbed the microphone again and said: *"We're carrying on with a strike in solidarity!"*. But the broadcasting system was already switched off. And then the women – Ewa Osowska, Alina Pienkowska and Mrs Ania [Walentynowicz] ran to the gates, to turn people back into the Shipyard. [27]

Alina Pienkowska:

I can remember the scene to this day: thousands of people on the bridge out of the Shipyard. I persuaded the guards to close the gates and began to explain that the strike on the other gates had been extended and I called on them to strike in solidarity with their colleagues. That worked – the crowd turned back from the gate. Of course, there were three gentlemen carrying brief cases who shouted: *"We're leaving!"*, but they were quickly kicked out of the gate. [19]

Photo: Grzegorz Nawrocki

Strikers on the walls of the Shipyard

Krzysztof Bobiński (journalist, "Financial Times" correspondent):

I was standing by Gate No. 3. The people leaving were mainly older people. It was clear they had had enough. They considered that they had achieved what they had set out to gain. They changed and wanted to go home for the weekend, to their families and children. It became clear that those who remained in the Shipyard were quite young people. [...] Saturday afternoon was a strike by 20-year olds. I wasn't sure that it would last – for that very reason. [17]

Bogdan Borusewicz:

People were going home the richer by 1,500 zloties. A strange situation evolved – the strike was supposedly over, but we stayed on inside, the police could have entered any moment, because there were not many of us there... That night was the worst. [27]

Zbigniew Trybek (photographer):

When I went into the Shipyard, shipyard workers were busy rubbing the numbers off their safety helmets. In 1970 they had been identified by these numbers. And subsequently harassed. Now they knelt, sat and rubbed out those numbers before my very eyes, using razor blades or sanding paper. [...] Photographs were their biggest fear. [17]

Photo: Zbigniew Trybek

The MKS in talks. From left: Zbigniew Kobyliński, Bogdan Borusewicz, Andrzej Gwiazda, Joanna Duda-Gwiazda, Alina Pienkowska

Extract from the first communiqué of the Inter-factory Strike Committee:

The aim of the Inter-factory Strike Committee (MKS) is the co-ordination of demands and strike action of factories and companies. [...] The text of the demands and terms, mutually agreed by the strike committees, has been formulated. It has been decided to continue the strike until such time as the demands and terms put forward by the workforces are satisfied. The MKS is empowered to undertake talks with central government.

Janusz Kołodziejski (journalist):

In the afternoon, a rumour began to circulate that an attack was to be made on the Shipyard that night. There were about 500 people left in the empty Lenin Shipyard. You could feel the enormous determination of these people. Conversations did not take place, as before, in an atmosphere of hope but in dread that this is where we would die like dogs. [17]

Photo: Bogusław Nieznalski

Bread for the strikers. First from right: Andrzej Karandziej; centre: Bogdan Borusewicz; first from left: Leszek Zborowski

Mieczysław Szuta (welder, Northern Shipyard):

Sometime after 4 p.m. a communiqué was read out, to say that they had come to an agreement in the Gdańsk Shipyard and that at 6 p.m. the workforce would leave the Shipyard. Some fifteen minutes, or so, later, Anna Walentynowicz arrived. She made a short speech, in which she exhorted us not to lose heart but to continue the strike. She said that the next day would be a big test for us.

At about 6 p.m. a man in dark glasses arrived from the Gdańsk Shipyard, a member of KOR, and our Strike Committee refused him the microphone. He said we should not give up, that most of the crew of the Gdańsk Shipyard had left for home but that a few thousand people had remained, in sympathy with us. He was cheered at that point. Hearing the clapping, our Committee put forward that we should not be friendly to this man as he represents KOR and that the people who have stayed on in the Shipyard are fighting for political aims and their own good. For several days after that there was to be a breakdown in relations between the two Shipyards.

A moment later we heard shouting: *"Cops! Cops!"*. The crowd immediately arose and rushed off in the direction of the "Stocznio-wiec" ("Shipyard Worker") Stadium, carrying stones, sticks and anything else that was handy. Apparently, someone had seen a militiaman near the fence on the Shipyard territory. They looked everywhere for him: under the wagons, in the tall grass, among the expanded polystyrene, but they didn't find anyone. [20]

Photo: Zbigniew Trybek

Photo: Chris Niedenthal/FORUM

Extract from a meeting of the Politburo of the Central Committee of the Polish United Workers Party:

Comrade Edward Gierek:

It would be wise to inform some of the Western diplomats about the situation in Gdańsk, but on a descending note – that the situation resulted from changes intended to tidy up the economy, but that, in a few cases, it was caused by the diversionary tactics of Radio Free Europe and we have had to deal with acts of terrorism (aggressive groups forcing people to stop work). We did not resort to force but we will remember this.   [24]

Extract from a leaflet signed by the Management of the Gdańsk Shipyard:

Who betrayed whom?
Who is lying?
Who needs this and why?
What are the political aims of the organisers of this whole action to keep part of the workforce in the Shipyard?
Why do they insult and demean those who, in accordance with the agreement, wanted to leave the Shipyard peacefully, and resume work as normal - let us ponder this calmly.

Extract from report of the City Commander of the Civil Militia in Gdańsk:

You can still observe extended shopping being carried out in food shops; in the main people are buying bread, buck-wheat, flour and all sorts of tinned produce and potatoes. Long queues are forming outside bakeries and greengrocers. Whatever amount of bread is delivered is immediately sold out. I would point out that, yesterday, 95 thousand more loaves of bread were bought than normal.

[...] In conversations carried on by people queuing in front of food shops, you can hear comments in support of the strike.   [4]

Photo: Maciej Osiecki

One of the first conditions for beginning talks is the restoration of telephone communication.

The demands of the striking workforce, represented by the Inter-factory Strike Committee, are as follows:

1. The recognition of Free Trade Unions, independent of both Party and employers, in accordance with the ratification by the Polish People's Republic of the 87th Convention of the International Labour Organisation concerning free unions.
2. Guarantee the right to strike and guarantee immunity for strikers and those assisting them.
3. Ensure the right of free speech, free press and publication, as guaranteed by the Constitution of the Polish People's Republic and by the same token not repress independent publishers and allow representatives of all faiths access to mass media.
4. a) Restore previous rights to:
   – people sacked from work following the strikes of 1970 and 1976,
   – students suspended from institutions of higher education for their views;
   b) Release all political prisoners (including Edmund Zadrożyński, Jan Kozłowski and Marek Kozłowski);
   c) Abolish repression for personal convictions.
5. Release information in the public media about the setting up of the Inter-factory Strike Committee, and publish its demands.
6. Undertake realistic action aimed at bringing the country out of the crisis situation, by:
   a) Supplying the public with full information about the state of the social and economic situation;
   b) Enabling all sections of society and all social levels to participate in discussions on the programme of reforms.
7. Pay all employees taking part in the strike at a paid holiday rate for the duration of the strike, from CRZZ (Central Trade Union Board) funds.
8. Raise the basic pay of every employee by 2,000 zloties per month, as compensation for recent price rises.
9. Guarantee automatic pay rises in line with price rises and inflation.
10. Satisfy the demands of the home food market and release only surplus stock for export.
11. Abolish special pricing and hard currency sales on the so-called domestic export market.
12. Recruit management staff on the basis of qualifications held and not party allegiance, and remove special privileges from the MO (Civil Militia), the SB (Security Police) and party officials through:
    – levelling out family allowances,
    – eliminating privileged shopping, etc.
13. Introduce rationing – food vouchers for meat and food products (until market stability is achieved).
14. Reduce retirement age for women to 50 and for men to 55, or on completion of 30 years' work in the Polish People's Republic for women and 35 years for men, irrespective of age.
15. Level out pensions and benefits from the old portfolio in line with current payments.
16. Improve working conditions in the Health Service, thus ensuring full medical care for working people.
17. Ensure adequate creche facilities and nursery school places for the children of working women.
18. Introduce paid maternity leave lasting three years for bringing up children.
19. Reduce waiting lists for housing.
20. Increase expense allowances from 40 zloties to 100 zloties, with a bonus for periods spent away from home.
21. Introduce work-free Saturdays throughout the year. Compensate workers in continuous cycle processes and [miners] on a 4-shift system, for missing out on free Saturdays by giving them additional holidays or other leave in lieu.

Gdynia Shipyard free printing press   Inter-factory Strike Committee

17-08-1980

Sunday

- *Workers return to the Gdańsk Shipyard in the morning.*
- *On the recommendation of the Inter-factory Strike Committee, all public services in the city are to return to normal duties; there is an appeal to the authorities of the Triple City of Gdańsk, Gdynia and Sopot to ban the sale of alcohol; no alcohol is allowed on the premises of any striking factory.*
- *The Authorities form a Commission to "look into the demands and grievances of the workforces and the problems of the Coastal Provinces", headed by the Deputy Prime Minister Tadeusz Pyka.*

Eugeniusz Możejewski (turner, "Nauta" Repair Shipyard, a member of the Inter--factory Strike Committee):

We worked on the formulation of our demands together, until the early hours. As morning broke, we decided to take a much needed rest. We lay down to sleep on chairs. As a result of the stress we were under and the rumours which were circulating, my colleague who was sleeping next to me, dreamt that the Russians were attacking us. He jumped up from his chair in his sleep and began to run to the door but tripped suddenly on his shoelace. He quickly picked himself up and ran out of the building where he came to.   [20]

Bogdan Borusewicz:

The demands were formulated in such a way that they dictated the tactical form of the negotiations. From the most important point to the easiest – and that's how they were to be tackled. Even if, for tactical reasons, the first point was omitted and left for later, then you would still have to return to it as to the main point.

Free trade unions was the maximum that we could hope to achieve. When, during the night, Tadeusz Szczudłowski of the Movement for the Defence of Human and Civil Rights added free parliamentary elections as one of the demands, then in the morning, after a short discussion, I had to cross it out. I also changed the demand for "an end to censorship" into "a restriction on censorship". It was important that the Soviets were not given a pretext for intervention, as in Czechoslovakia in 1968.

Those 21 demands – with their leading item – became a template for the strikers – for those factories which did not have their own team of opposition activists. There was a handful of us here and thanks to this we were able to steer this huge movement.

Bernard Pogorzelski (Gdynia Shipyard worker):

In our department, we very quickly knocked together a large wooden cross, a temporary altar was set up on a trailer, the pavement was swept and planks were used to make benches. [...] We awaited that Sunday with enthusiasm and when the moment came and the orchestra gave the signal for the beginning of Mass, a huge crowd of people dressed in their workday boiler-suits stood up and began to

Photo: Bogusław Nieznalski

sing loudly. It was very moving. I felt my throat constrict and tears came to my eyes. Had any of us ever dreamt that we would live to see such times and experience such a moving moment in the grounds of our Shipyard? [20]

Extract from Father Hilary Jastak's
sermon (Holy Mass in the Gdynia Shipyard):

The President of the City of Gdynia announced to my superior at the Redemptorist Fathers that what you are doing is sabotage and he warned me not to go to you in pursuit of my holy duties.

There is some sort of misunderstanding here. [...] The demand for human rights and truth, participation in spreading and supporting various forms of self-determination of working people is guaranteed not only by natural law, God's law but also by positive, international law laid down in Helsinki, as well as by the constitutional law of the Polish People's Republic.

[...] All forms of the law stand behind you, in support of your stand and your just demands.

[...] It cannot be denied that your action was prompted by your concern for the future of the Nation – which the Prime Minister questions – concern for its sovereignty, for freedom of speech, thought and religion, that your actions result from your honest and best intentions, which are deserving of support and respect. He, who suspects your motives, or claims that you are not driven by honest and good intentions, is nothing but a slanderer. [8]

Photo: Archives of the National Commission of NSZZ "Solidarność"

Father Hilary Jastak

Father Hilary Jastak:

And then a helicopter hovered over us and leaflets were scattered. However, nobody made a move to bend down and pick them up. I sensed then the meaning of unity. Nobody could be sure that this eucharistic offering might not be brutally interrupted by a show of force. Many thousands of people participated in the Sacrament but we only had two thousand hosts, so they had to be broken into half, into quarters, into tiny pieces and crumbs, to ensure there was enough to go round. [33]

Photo: Bogusław Nieznalski

The Gdańsk Shipyard; centre: Tadeusz Szczudłowski

Edmund Soszyński (Gdańsk Shipyard worker):

From the early hours, people from Gdańsk, Gdynia and Sopot began to mass in front of the second gate, while the grounds of the Shipyard remained silent and empty, except for a few people who were putting the finishing touches to the decoration of the altar. The shipyard workers in their various departments were also making preparations – they were shaving and putting on clean overalls. That was how they wished to emphasise their faith in God and in their country. Just before Holy Mass there were some shipyard workers who could not believe the change which had come about and even some who claimed that tanks would appear during Mass. But these words were without meaning because, as the hour of 9 a.m. neared, there was an atmosphere of victory

and peace, which had been so lacking on Saturday 16th August. [20]

Andrzej Kołodziej (Gdynia Shipyard):

The workforce demanded the unequivocal removal of the whole of the management team from the Shipyard, despite the fact that, earlier on, these same people had been afraid that, in the event of the removal of the management, we would be exposed to possible militia action.

[...] The Director said he was handing the Shipyard over to the strike committee but, as he has strong ties with the Shipyard, he wants to remain inside even [should he be] shut in. The people decided that the management could stay but under lock and key. There were immediate volunteers for guard duty. There must have been some five hundred of them, each of them happy to stand guard over the Director and the Party Secretary. [25]

Jerzy Durlik (Gdańsk Shipyard worker):

We spent all Sunday in the vicinity of Gate No. 2. In the evening a member of the duty squad approached us, asking whether we could go to the Kaszubskie Shore to investigate, as suspicious movements had been detected on the other side of the canal and a rumour had spread that an attack was to be launched from there. [...]

Once we had reached the spot – by the canal along the fence between our Shipyard and the "Repair Yard", we suddenly realised that, should there really be an attack, we were quite helpless. The next thought which came to mind was: if there is calm inside the Shipyard, if there is no sabotage, then there

Strikers in the Gdańsk Shipyard

Photo: Maciej Billewicz/PAI-EXPO

are no grounds for militia or army intervention; our first aim must be to ensure that no-one from outside is allowed to get into the Shipyard in order to carry out any acts of sabotage or to provoke any incidents. [20]

Tadeusz Knade (journalist from "Słowo Powszechne"):

I spent Saturday and Sunday in the Gdańsk Shipyard. I felt it expedient to let Warsaw know about the strikers' programme, their demands and, as soon as their provisional list had been accepted, I got hold of a typed copy and immediately ran to the Gdańsk Branch of "Słowo". Unfortunately, it turned out that I was cut off from the Warsaw editorial offices, the telex and telephones were dead. So all I could do was... bang my head against the wall. I remembered December 70. I realised that nothing had changed. I was hampered in my actions, my journalism fettered. And at that moment, in effect, I ceased to be a journalist. [17]

Photo: Zbigniew Trybek

Extract from minutes of meeting of the City Executive Committee of the Polish United Workers Party in Gdynia:

Comrade Jarosław Polski (Secretary of the City Committee of the PZPR in Gdańsk):

[...] It is being said all over the place that a general strike is to be organised for 18th August throughout the country. It would seem, therefore, that nothing will stop them before Monday. [...]

There was a demand that Mass be celebrated in the Gdańsk Shipyard and in the Paris Commune Shipyard [in Gdynia]. A procession was planned but, after consultation with the bishops in Gdańsk and Pelplin, the Governor of Gdańsk refused permission for a procession. At 11 p.m. a delegation from the Strike Committee arrived in the Provincial Committee offices of the Polish United Workers Party in Gdańsk. They talked with Comrade Fiszbach and he agreed to their holding Masses. The appearance of the priest in Gdańsk was perfectly correct, but in the Paris Commune Shipyard it was out of order and intended to foment sedition. [3]

Extract from speech made by Tadeusz Fiszbach to the inhabitants of the Coastal Provinces:

The working discussions have turned into constant demonstrations, with the participation of people who are in no way connected with the Shipyard. [...]

We all work for ourselves. We should not, therefore, make this work more difficult for ourselves because then we work against our own interests and make everyday life even more difficult than it already is.

[...] The inhabitants of Gdańsk and Gdynia still bear painful memories of the events of December 1970. Mindful of that time, let us retain our common sense and responsibility for every decision, for every step we take.

Extract from a report by the City Commander of the Civil Militia in Gdańsk:

At about 10.30 a.m., at the end of the Mass [in the Gdańsk Shipyard], the priest celebrating the Mass appealed to those gathered there to leave in a calm manner. At that, eight shipyard workers approached the cross, cut off the ropes binding it to the gate and when the left side of the gate was opened they carried it through the gate and out of the Shipyard to the place where the monument is to be built. [...]

Towards the end of the celebrations Lech Wałęsa spoke, lifted aloft by several shipyard workers, and declared that the strike would be continued until such time as the demands of the smaller factories were met. [...] He underlined that he had been the first to go in and would be the last to leave. The crowd sang "may he live a hundred years". [4]

Extract from telexed information from the Central Committee of the Polish United Workers Party to Provincial Committees:

Information received from the Provincial Committee regarding the situation in the Triple City indicates an escalation of demands, the inclusion of political slogans; we are passing on to you the main demands currently being formulated in Gdańsk and Gdynia – mainly in the Paris Commune Shipyard and in the Lenin Shipyard. We are also letting you have some points raised in the argumentation, which may be of use to Party activists in their argumentation. [1]

3 x TAK DLA POLSKI SOCJALISTYCZNEJ POLSKI SPRAWIEDLIWEJ POLSKI PRACOWITEJ

Photo: Maciej Osiecki

Slogan: 3 x YES for a SOCIALIST Poland, a JUST Poland, a HARD-WORKING Poland

18-08-1980

Monday

- The Inter-factory Strike Committee (MKS) encompasses 156 enterprises; an MKS Presidium is set up.
- Strike begins in the "Parnica" Repair Shipyard and in the Warski Shipyard in Szczecin; a Szczecin Inter-factory Strike Committee is formed, under the leadership of Marian Jurczyk; a list of 36 demands is announced.
- An overnight Plenum of the Central Committee of the Polish United Workers Party takes place in Gdańsk, with the participation of Stanisław Kania and Tadeusz Pyka.

Citizens of Gdańsk, Gdynia and Sopot !!!
In view of mass misinformation we wish to inform you of the current strike situation
strikes continue !

Currently approx. 2,000 factories and enterprises in the Triple City are on strike. They are sit-in strikes. An Inter-factory Strike Committee has been formed, with Headquarters in the Gdańsk Lenin Shipyard and it is our sole representative in talks with the authorities.
Factory Strike Committees are maintaining order in the workplaces.
Full order is being maintained and there are no incidents, you need not worry about us.
WE WILL ENDURE !!!
THE INTER-FACTORY STRIKE COMMITTEE

GDYNIA Shipyard Free Printing Press
18.08.80

Leaflet from the government side:

Workers of the Gdańsk Lenin Shipyard!
Two days ago you left your place of work, knowing that your demands had been met. [...] Whilst you were having a well-deserved rest at home, a group of your colleagues, incited by people who do not have your welfare and that of your families in mind, announced a sympathy strike - in spite of the decisions of the Strike Committee, thus breaking the agreement which had been reached. This strikes at the very basic foundations of our system and the life of the country.

Bogdan Borusewicz:

On Monday 18th August thousands of people who had left the strike on Saturday arrived at the Shipyard. I had given instructions earlier to let them in. Just before seven o'clock, I went down to the gate and saw a crowd standing some small distance away. I realised that these people were not entering because they were being jeered at by the strikers, having to undergo a "path of shame" — to the accompaniment of jeers such as "traitors" and "scabs" and other epithets, and beating with rolled newspapers, sometimes even being spat on. I put a stop to that. We opened the gates. At first we did not know what might happen, it was something of a risk. If they were, indeed, to resume work then the strike would be broken (the broadcasting system was still in management hands, and used to sow dissension among the shipyard workers). In fact, they all re-joined the strike. [37]

Strike in the Warski Shipyard in Szczecin. Sign reads: We support Gdańsk, Gdynia and fact[ory]…

Jerzy Durlik (Gdańsk Shipyard worker):

After breakfast we stayed in the vicinity of our departments and at about 10 o'clock one of our colleagues arrived and told us that the foreman was waiting for us on the shop floor. A strange sight awaited us on the shop floor: all the lights were on, the charge-hand was working on the bending machine, a welder was welding, at the other end of the shop floor there were two arcs of electric light from the arc welders. I met the foreman and asked what was going on. *"Going on?"* he asked, *"it's about time to get on*

with work", to which I answered that, if the majority began work then I would, too. He then said that we have to start with individuals, but I told him I would not be that individual.   [20]

A worker (Szczecin Shipyard):

I have no idea who made the first move. A group of shipyard workers marched through several departments calling on people to strike, a crowd then gathered in the vicinity of the main gate. There were some 1,500, or perhaps 2,000 people there. [...] We all stood there and people shouted loudly. Each one wanted to out-shout the next, some were trying to deafen their own qualms. The Director of the Shipyard arrived but was told that he was not competent to undertake such discussions, and the presence of someone with greater authority was demanded.   [21]

Piotr Halberszdat (journalist, Polish Television News):

Wałęsa, standing on a battery-powered truck, was shouting into a megaphone: *"Sir, we demand that management gives us the use of the broadcasting system. You have 15 minutes to make up your mind, then we're going in and placing you under arrest!".* [...] [Later] Wałęsa went to see the Director. He was gone a few minutes. [...] He came back visibly dejected. He took the megaphone and said: *"I did not arrest Mr Gniech. I just couldn't do it".* He also said that he should leave because he is not fit to lead the strike; after all, he had been arrested himself on so many occasions and knew how it was done but he could not bring himself to do it to another human being. [...] It was very amusing and wonderful to see how all the workers cheered him up: *"Don't worry, Leszek. No point in worrying about a little shit".*   [17]

Lech Wałęsa in front of the Management building

Andrzej Kołodziej (Gdynia Shipyard):

The communications systems, printing press and broadcasting system taken from the works security were now in the hands of the strikers. Three times a day 8,000 meals were distributed, food provisions were secured, and the security system was working well. [...]

Special care was taken to ensure that alcohol was not smuggled onto the premises. [...] A strict register was kept of all the people leaving and coming back into the Shipyard.

Being in charge of all this, from Thursday through to Monday morning, I didn't even have time for a nap. On my last legs, I managed to sit down in some armchair and fell asleep. After half an hour I was woken up, as something important had again to be seen to.   [25]

Photo: Zbigniew Trybek

Photo: Zbigniew Trybek

Shipyard in Gdynia; top: food intended for various departments; bottom: a polystyrene hut

Andrzej Ropelewski (Gdynia):

In the afternoon I went out with our driver and drove to the Repair Yard, to the Marine Railway Station and the Paris Commune Shipyard. Everywhere, the entry gates were barricaded with trailers and manned by people wearing arm-bands. At the junction of Czechosłowacka and Marchlewski Streets, a piece of paper was fixed to a post, and bore the

following message:

"Attention all Communarders!

All those who wish to enter the Paris Commune Shipyard,

will be allowed in, provided they fulfil the following requirements:

– they want to join us,

– they are not managers,

– they have been on holiday or on sick leave and can prove this.

We appeal for order at the gate. The strike continues.

Strike Committee"

Józef Kuczma (Gdynia Shipyard worker):

I meet up with the secretary of our departmental Party organisation during a discussion with the manager and some other people. He returned to work today after a holiday. He entered the Shipyard grounds on production of a pass, like everyone coming back from holiday. He says we have to talk to people, to persuade them. As usual, when I hear such talk, I walk out.

[...]

I watch "First" [First Secretary], led by a group of people. He is in the middle, next to Kołodziej. He doesn't look happy; hands in his pockets, his briefcase hanging from one arm. His eyes are fixed on the ground. They approach a trolley. Kołodziej gets up on the trolley and introduces "First":

"Listen to me, all you shipyard workers. Here is one of those who takes your money. You work to keep such idle hands, while they sit behind their desks and try to steer you by remote control".

At that point he pulls "First" onto the trolley.

"Shipyard workers, what shall we do with this man? [...] Judge him yourselves."

The crowd roars with laughter and whistles. Someone dashes up to the trolley and spits

towards "First", somebody else shouts: *"Out of the gate with him, feet first!"*. There are shouts of: throw him out, we don't want his like here; the whistles and jeers seem unending. Asked what he has to say for himself, "First" remains silent and only shrugs his shoulders.

[...] Eventually, to the accompaniment of jeers, whistles and general insults, "First" is led out of the gate by the strikers' security guards.   [20]

Workforce Representative Committee of the Gdańsk Refinery Plants to the Governor of the Gdańsk Province:

The Workforce Representative Committee of the Gdańsk Refinery Plants hereby makes a categorical demand, on its own behalf and that of the workforces of other enterprises taking part in strike action, that shops and kiosks selling alcohol be closed for the duration of the strike for obvious reasons.

Krzysztof Bobiński (correspondent of the London "Financial Times"):

On 18th August, Gierek gave his first speech. I went to Kuroń's home that day. He was in something of a state. Hysterical, tired, nervy. He was extremely worried by the fact that Gierek was not prepared to compromise and was convinced that this speech would anger people so much that they would take to the streets and riots would follow. Part of the time we talked, part of the time he gave an interview for Danish radio.

A movement had been born in the Shipyard, which had far outstripped even the most daring hopes of the opposition.   [17]

The Presidium of Inter-factory Strike Committee

Photo: Zbigniew Trybek

Extract from an Appeal by KSS "KOR" and the Editorial Staff of "The Worker":

All the strikes are taking place in an atmosphere of calm and seriousness. The workers' demonstration shows due responsibility for the fate of the nation. However, some of the strikers and members of the Strike Committees are being harassed by functionaries of the Security Police. Their families are often subject to blackmail, their homes searched, they are constantly watched and sometimes even arrested: they are subjected to threats and to provocation. The same is true, to an even greater extent, of all those people collecting information about the strike. This information is blocked, telephone lines are cut, millions of zloties are spent on invigilation equipment and staff, who eavesdrop, spy and conduct investigations. The authorities are once again trying to stifle the truth and put down independent civic initiative with police methods. This is proof of a lack of responsibility for the fate of the country. Wherever the authorities continue to try to cheat us, or where the political police are involved, either openly or by stealth, in all these places negotiations should be broken off.

Ewa Milewicz (KSS "KOR"):

Beginning of Gierek's speech – the conference room is empty. Wałęsa, annoyed by this insubordination, calls the delegates to the room and speaks of their "political duty" to listen to what Gierek has to say. The delegates complain: What sense can he make? What difference does it make – he won't agree to the demands, anyway, so we'll just go on striking. Why bother to fill our heads with rubbish – let him speak to Party members. *"He'll probably ask us to help him"* – laughs someone beside me.

Wałęsa about Gierek: *"We're not interested, we have our 21 demands"*.				[7]

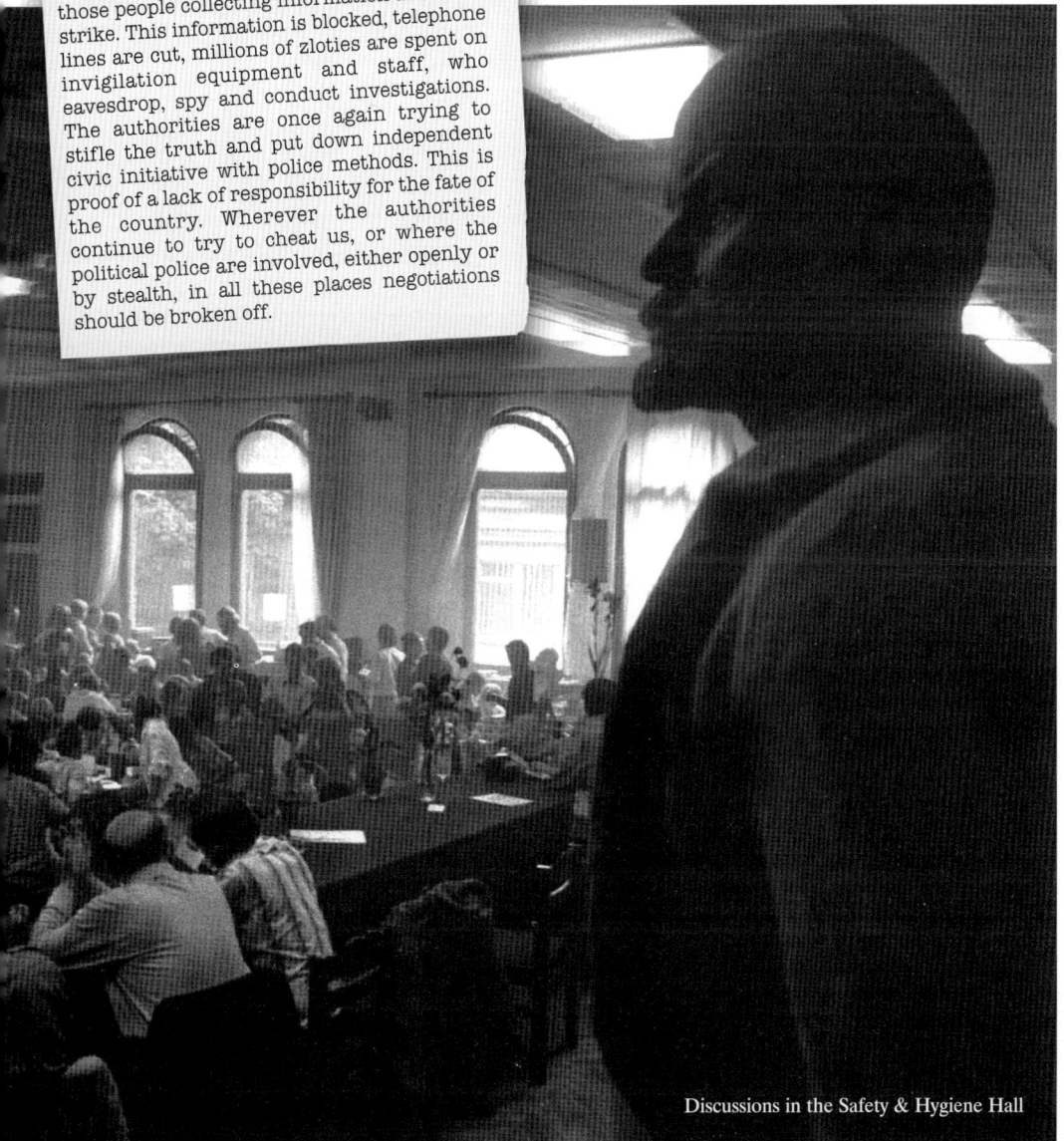

Discussions in the Safety & Hygiene Hall

Extract from information sent to the Central Committee concerning Jacek Kuroń's interview, broadcast on Swedish television:

On 18th August, Swedish television broadcast an interview given to a British radio correspondent, in its news broadcast. [...]

J. Kuroń's statement (broadcast in Polish):

We are on a very sharp bend. This movement demands basic rights for society and, at the same time, it's the drowning nation's only hope. [...] The movement is trying to save the country, an attempt made in spite of the authorities. We now face the imminent danger of overthrowing the authorities, because that would be natural progression. But the authorities must not be overthrown, guarded as they are by Russian tanks.

We must, therefore, walk this tight rope, organise ourselves against the authorities but not overthrow them. This widespread movement, a trade union movement [...] and all these associations must, step by step, force through reforms leading to democracy while, at the same time, not overthrowing the totalitarian, pro-Soviet facade of the system. [1]

Extract from a meeting the Politburo of the Central Committee of the Polish United Workers Party:

Comrade Edward Gierek:

The situation is bad. One positive aspect is that there are no appeals to take to the streets. [...]

What can we do, under the circumstances, to get through to the Party and the Nation? After consultation with my comrades, I propose that rather than call a Plenum we should make a radio and television broadcast. Issue a statement saying that the Prime Minister's Office has taken stock of the socio-political situation in the country, and then I will go on air and face the cameras. The tone of my speech – should be a tone of dialogue, dividing the working classes from the extremists, with an accent on the principles of socialism, on alliances, etc. [...]

Comrade Stanisław Kania:

A speech is a good idea – but it must be good because if we lose this hand, then what happens next? [24]

Photo: Piotr Wójcik, The Library, Institute of Literary Research, Polish Academy of Sciences

Billboard slogan: What are we fighting for, where are we going – Socialism

Extract from Edward Gierek's speech broadcast on radio and television:

Respected Citizens! Countrymen! The events of the last few weeks, and particularly of the last few days, fill us all with deep concern. The interruption of work in so many factories, which now spreads region by region, affects the natural life cycle, disrupts production, gives rise to tension.

[...]

We can understand how the atmosphere of tension and emotion can affect even the most honest of people. It is, however, our duty to state with absolute assertiveness that no activities, which strike at the principles of political and social order in Poland, can be tolerated.

[...]

There are boundaries, which may not be crossed by anyone. They are set by the Polish status quo. A sense of responsibility for the fate of the Fatherland. [8]

Jerzy Kołodziejski (Governor of Gdańsk Province):

Reality came as a shock to the authorities. Within three days practically the whole of Gdańsk was on strike, the entire province. We were aware that the strike action was becoming increasingly organised, that this organised workers' protest is notable for its ideal calm and restraint, which is especially evident in the city. Regretfully – as a representative of the authorities – I had to admit that we had undoubtedly lost control of the province. [...] Memories of the December Events served to prevent any violent or hasty decisions. [13]

Extract from speech made by Stanisław Kania at the Plenum of the Provincial Committee of the Polish United Workers Party in Gdańsk:

The current difficult situation must be resolved by political means. They are decisive. That is the only way forward.

Extract from status report from the Provincial Headquarters of the Civil Militia to the Ministry of the Interior:

In the Gdańsk Repair Yard [...] as a result of the fact that the Inter-factory Strike Committee selected 8 delegates from KSS "KOR" and WZZ to take part in negotiations with the authorities, representatives of the Yard decided not to put forward their own representative to take part in the delegation. They stated that they wished to have nothing to do with KOR and WZZ. A similar stance was taken by the Strike Committee in the Northern Shipyard. [4]

Extract from telex information from the Provincial Committee in Katowice to the Central Committee of the Polish United Workers Party:

During the discussions, the workers demand that the authorities undertake concrete action to prevent lawlessness and disruptive action by groups of hooligans, to uphold respect for the law and to ensure that all citizens are able to carry on working in peace.

Zygmunt Banaszak, a miner and cutter-loaderman from the KWK "Barbara-Chorzów" Mine, speaking on behalf of his work colleagues, said: *"People are of one mind – it is time to put a stop to all this trouble-making. There's no place for people like that in our society, because they pose a very decided threat; they disrupt the working patterns of those who want to work honestly and properly".*

[...] We hear of incidents of negative attitudes towards the people of the Katowice Province [...] in personal contacts and conversations, some people even complain that here, in Śląsk (Silesia) we have good working conditions. [1]

Extract from a cryptogram from the Deputy Director of the Operational Office to the Commander of the Civil Militia Officer Training School in Słupsk:

On the orders of the Deputy Minister of Internal Affairs, Lieutenant General B. Stachura, on 18.08.1980 at 22:00 hours relocate 180 cadets from the school, together with the officer corps by means of regular [?] vehicle carrier, putting them under the command of the Provincial Commander of the Civil Militia in Gdańsk.

The force should be equipped as for riot control purposes, in field uniforms, one unit with tear gas equipment, no fire-arms. [4]

19-08-1980

Tuesday

- *The Gdańsk Inter-factory Strike Committee now counts 250 member enterprises (including companies from Elbląg, Pruszcz Gdański, Starogard and Tczew).*
- *Strike action in Szczecin is spreading.*
- *Representatives of 17 striking factories from Gdańsk, Gdynia and Sopot, including the Repair Yard and the Northern Shipyard, undertake their own discussions with Tadeusz Pyka's Commission.*

From a Statement made by the Inter-factory Strike Committee:

We are awaiting the arrival of the people from central government. [...] On behalf of the work-forces which we represent, we state our wish to return to work as soon as possible, but to do so as fully-fledged citizens, as true joint participants of our workplaces.

Marianna Waliszewska (old-age pensioner, Gdańsk):

"My strike" began for me on 19th August. On that day I had my reward for all the humiliation of the past years, for all the moments of elation which came to nothing, for all our unfulfilled hopes, for the inability to speak the truth, for the tears, the drudgery and the helplessness of the December events of 1970. All this was rewarded by the light in my son's eyes and face when he came home and said to me: *"Mother, we're joining the strike, I'm going to the Shipyard with a delegation to register our participation"*. [20]

Kazimierz Małek (mechanical technician, "Ustka" Shipyard):

The town is beginning to empty. The hordes of holiday-makers are making haste to leave Ustka. The inhabitants are in constant dread of force being used by the Civil Militia and the Security Police. Nor are we free of this dread. After all, in Słupsk – not far from here – we have the well-known Militia "hatchery", not to mention numerous army units; what chance does a shipyard worker, armed with a spade handle taken from the store-room, have against them? [20]

Photo: Bogusław Nieznalski

Daily prayers were run by (from left): Bożena Rybicka and Magdalena Modzelewska of the Young Poland Movement. Photo shows them kneeling with Lech Wałęsa.

34

Extract from the diary of Regina Dąbrowska (on holiday in Jurata):

There's just one thing on my mind: how am I to get the girls home safely? We are leaving tomorrow morning. We have no choice — there's only one train, one route and that goes through the Triple City.

That night was very long and sleepless. I paced up and down and thought: we'll be travelling all day. We should be in the Triple City by about midday. What's going on there? Have there been any shootings, or not (so far, there always have been). When I bought the reserved seats in Warsaw I made sure that the girls got window seats. Now, I'll have to make them crouch or lie down on the floor. [...]

We're approaching the Triple City, I'm ready in case I have to defend the children, I'm so afraid for them. [...]

We're entering the Triple City and what I see quite takes my breath away. People are standing and sitting on the walls, in their windows, on gateways, there are flags and banners everywhere; at factory gates women are passing things to the men. There is calm, peace and daring. It's quite incredible, new and wonderful.

Ewa Milewicz:

Every day some one hundred new enterprises join us — every enterprise has two delegates. In theory, only one of the delegates takes part in the talks, while the other keeps up the morale of the workforce but, in reality, both are interested to see what is going on in the conference room. [...] Since Tuesday, various delegations to the Inter-factory Strike Committee have been arriving, bearing words of solidarity. Everybody who can and wants to is in sympathy with us: factories, companies, cities and towns, provinces, ladies returning from holiday... [7]

Lech Wałęsa:

During the meetings of the Inter-factory Strike Committee, held in the Health & Safety conference room, I immediately realised that people were too full of emotion, too over-excited to be able to conduct serious discussions and to undertake binding decisions. We had, as it was, a ritual: the doors would open, I walked down the middle to the table, set on a small podium, I turned round suddenly to face the audience, I was silent for a minute, then I would announce that I am opening the meeting of the Inter-factory Strike Committee and would propose that we sing the national anthem. Everybody in the hall stood up and sang the anthem. People who literally just minutes earlier had been preparing harsh words of the "we'll show them" type, were now accepting decisions taken in small working groups. [23]

Photo: Erazm Ciołek

Lech Wałęsa among the strikers

Janusz Jachnicki (employee of the Test Department of the Main Post Office in Gdynia):

On Tuesday I brought a tape recorder to work with me, as I had decided to set up a tap on the City Committee of the Polish United Workers Party in Gdynia. First, I swore my colleague from the Repair Department, with whom I worked, to secrecy.

After several telephone calls from informers, a man telephoned — they recognised each other by their voices and did not introduce themselves. The one who had telephoned read out a text about the support of the town's inhabitants for the strikers. It turned out that this was a speech by Tadeusz Fiszbach, the First Secretary of the Provincial Committee of the Polish United Workers Party in Gdańsk — and diametrically different to that presented officially. I passed on the tape to the Inter-

Photo: Aleksander Jałosiński

-factory Strike Committee; at the Shipyard, Bogdan Borusewicz decided they would print this in the strike bulletin.

Edward Appel (Gdańsk Shipyard):

It's almost midnight, we had spent most of our time till then playing cards – I don't think I've ever played so many rounds in one go. It's time to rest now. I make up a bed on the top of a desk using all the clothes, which have piled up in the locker. A lever-arch file wrapped in towels serves as a pillow. It's devilishly hard and to cap it all my legs hang over the end of the desk and I can't get comfortable. Then I accidentally knock a telephone to the floor. The noise wakes everybody...   [20]

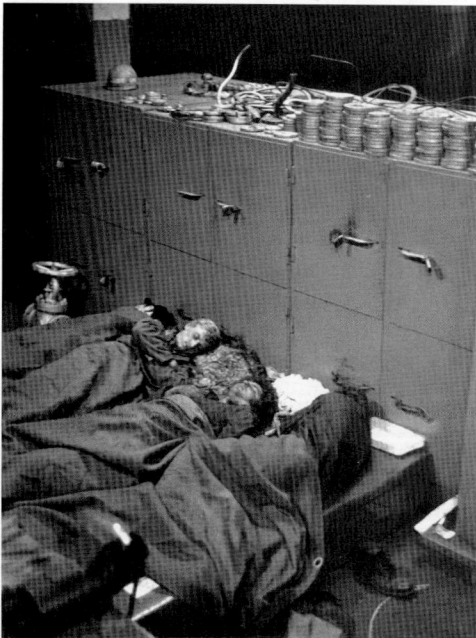

Photo: Zbigniew Trybek

Photo: Zbigniew Trybek

From a meeting of the City Executive Committee of the Provincial Committee of the Polish United Workers Party in Gdynia:

Stachowiak from the Paris Commune Shipyard (SKP) has given us information concerning the situation in the SKP. [...] The Strike Committees are led by clever people, so every hour is vital. The situation in the SKP must not be taken lightly. We understand the economic situation but we were not kept informed about it. Our adversaries, on the other hand, were fully informed. [...]

Hawrylewicz, an employee of the Paris Commune Shipyard: I am one of the people who had to leave the Shipyard. The situation in the SKP is tragic. The shipyard workers have been coerced. [...] Our people, i.e. members of the Polish United Workers Party are being thrown out of the Shipyard, they are being given demeaning jobs and tasks. The secretaries of the Factory Committees of the Polish United Workers Party are being arrested.   [3]

Extract from a report from the "Factory Strike Committees":

Strike Committees of 17 enterprises in the Triple City met with the Government Commission for the investigation of complaints and problems in the Gdańsk Coastal Provinces, headed by Deputy Prime Minister Tadeusz Pyka.

During a meeting held by the two parties, investigations were conducted into the demands of the striking work crews. Deputy Prime Minister Pyka accepted them and gave assurances that over 20 of the demands made would be fulfilled in the time designated. [...] The Government Commission guaranteed a considerable improvement in the provision of meat and other foodstuffs. An increase in housing construction will be assured in the Gdańsk Coastal Provinces by the building of two new construction plants.

Wojciech Giełżyński (journalist):

The negotiations went , more or less, like this: Deputy Prime Minister Pyka:

"You say there is no meat. OK. You'll get 60 tons. We'll import it!"

"But, Prime Minister, when will we get the meat?"

"I'll have to ask the Minister. Andrzej, when will we have the meat?" (this to Minister Jedynak)

"There won't be any, Mr Prime Minister."

"OK. Shut up! If we import it from the European Free Trade area, then we'll have it."

[...] He went on: "I know that you have difficulties with housing. OK, 120 families will be housed. I'll give you 2 construction plants. One producing concrete slabs, and the other producing nice little detached houses. Under a French licence. Does that make you happy?"
[11]

Fot. Adam Urbanek/ADM/PAP

Extract from a letter from the Secretarial Office of the Central Committee of the Polish United Workers Party to "all basal and branch Party organisations! To all Party Members!":

We must all realise that our safety and our independence are not given to us for all time. They are dependent entirely on the wisdom, discretion and unity of our nation, on its work and on its close knit adherence to the rule of the people. However, the tension in Gdańsk and in Gdynia have already given support to the West German revenge-seekers who do not hesitate to issue declarations saying that the events in Gdańsk and other towns in the Coastal Provinces are music to their revisionist ears. [1]

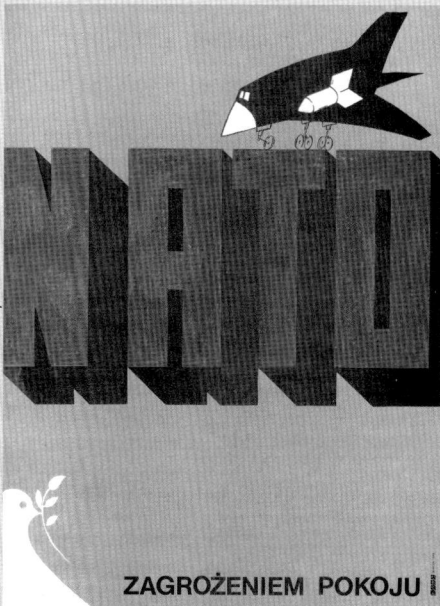

From the Collection of the Museum of Independence

ZAGROŻENIEM POKOJU

Slogan on poster: NATO – a threat to peace

Extracts from tapped radio conversations between officers of the Road Traffic Section of the Civil Militia, responsible for traffic control in the Gdańsk Shipyard vicinity:

"32 to 620. We have the TV here, they want to film a view of the Shipyard from the iron bridge, with a commentator, for "Panorama" [local Gdańsk Television programme]. We don't interfere?"

"Why should you interfere?!"

"Well, how do I know what they want?! You can't trust anybody any more." [9]

From a speech made by the Leader of the Cabinet of Ministers, Edward Babiuch, at the Plenum of the Provincial Committee of the Polish United Workers Party in Szczecin:

Comrades! [...] In many of the factories, with which we have recently been dealing, there have, unfortunately, been instances where we, members of the Party, have allowed ourselves to be taken unawares. If we keep close to the people, speak to them directly, show concern and are active, then I believe we can turn around this trend in the Szczecin area, we'll bring back calm and restore order... [35]

From a speech made by Janusz Brych, the First Secretary of the Provincial Committee of the Polish United Workers Party in Szczecin, at a Plenum of the Provincial Committee:

Yesterday, during the night and today we have been engaged in a series of discussions with various comrades. We have put the question directly: let's try and get things together, where are our Party tub-thumpers? The other side is carrying on discussions of this nature and we are to stand on the sidelines? I would like the Plenum of the Provincial Committee to make known its stand on the current state of the Party organisations. Comrades, we must use Party meetings to draw us closer together. We have 80 thousand members in the Szczecin Province. In the city of Szczecin there are some 40 thousand members. Are the directives contained in Comrade Gierek's speech not sufficient to improve the situation? [35]

From a situation report by the Provincial Headquarters of the Civil Militia in Gdańsk to the Ministry of the Interior:

The Bishops of Gdańsk and the Bishopric have expressed their concern and fear that the situation might escalate and lead to a physical confrontation between the strikers and the militia.

[...] As a result of investigative procedures carried out during services in selected churches throughout the Triple City and the Province, the conclusion has been reached that in the majority of cases the priests appeal to the congregations to pray for a successful resolution of this difficult situation. Especially active in this manner is Father Jankowski, in whose parish lie the Gdańsk Shipyard and other shipyards. He has frequently [...] persuaded the strikers to cut themselves off from the political tendencies, which the Inter-factory Strike Committee, led by provocateurs and political trouble-mongers, tries to enforce. [4]

20-08-1980

Wednesday

- *The talks held by Pyka's commission and the striking factories end in a fiasco. The strikers join the Inter-factory Strike Committee, which now counts 304 member enterprises.*
- *The Szczecin based Inter-factory Strike Committee is joined by factories and companies from Świnoujście; in total there are some 30 factories.*
- *Security Police arrest over twenty members and associates of KOR.*

Extract from a leaflet of the independent "Biuletyn Dolnośląski" ("Lower Silesia Bulletin") to the inhabitants of Lower Silesia:

We must not allow the Coastal Provinces to be isolated. There is but one Poland. We should recognise and publicly pronounce that the demands and needs of the shipyard workers are the needs and demands of all of us, that THEY ARE NOT AND WILL NOT BE ALONE. [...] We must organise ourselves in defence of the demands of the working people and in defence of the people who proclaim them.

Andrzej Jakubowski (Wrocław):

The wide-spread publication of the 21 demands of the Gdańsk Inter-factory Strike Committee – unfortunately not in the official media – has caused people to discard their pessimistic attitudes, based on previous sorry experience, which caused them to ask "what can I, a simple citizen, do, what can I change, what influence can I have, my protests won't make any difference anyway, and I have a wife and children to think of..."

Edward Appel (Gdańsk Shipyard):

The "Ruch" newsagent kiosks in the Shipyard are open. We buy morning papers – but there is nothing of note in them. The tone of some of the

Health and Safety Executive Room, Gdańsk Shipyard

Photo: Zbigniew Trybek

comments often makes one smile, in spite of everything. After all, things are not really the way they are presented in print. We are here, on the spot, and we feel and interpret the situation differently than it would appear from the newspaper reports. We realise that, as long as the editors of our newspapers do not have the freedom to write what they want, we will not be able to read the truth about ourselves in the newspapers. [20]

From a meeting of the Strike Committee of the Provincial Transport Company (WPK):

In the morning we had a proposition from Pyka that all four members of our Committee should get in a car and go the Provincial Committee for talks.

[...] What is it that the Provincial Committee really wants? To simply get rid of this Inter-factory Strike Committee? Why? They are afraid of unity, afraid of our strength. After all, unity is strength.

[...] Why are they so intent on WPK? It's simple, we – even though there's only a handful of us in comparison to other, huge, concerns – but we, we – and that means each and every one of us – can be seen. If transport

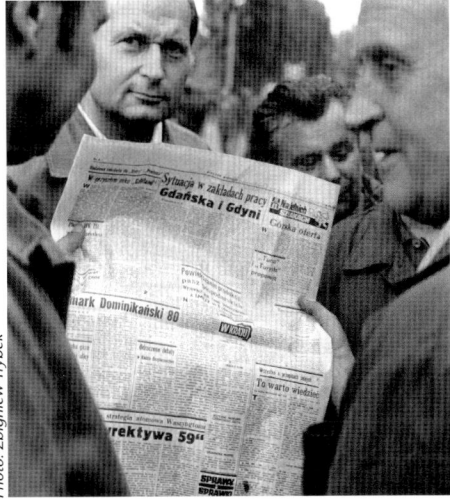

Photo: Zbigniew Trybek

stops then it is obvious to everybody. I'll bet my life on it that most people wake up in the morning and their first thought is to check, to look whether the bus is out on the street, whether the tram has started out on its route. And that keeps many people going, keeps their spirits up. [9]

From the evening talks of the Plenum of the Inter-factory Strike Committee:

"We are delegates from the Northern Shipyard. We have come to observe (*clapping*). We are with you always and will continue to be with you. And we will carry on with our strike as long as all the factories are on strike."

Bogdan Lis:

Ladies and gentlemen, it is now obvious not only that the plan to divide us has fizzled out before it got going, but the government has quite literally made a fool of itself.
[...]

A Delegate from a Milk Production Plant in Gdańsk-Maćki:

The management tried to form a two-man delegation, which was to go to the Gdańsk Provincial Governor for talks. We got the work force together, presented everyone with the facts, the crew did not agree and so we came here. Despite that, the Director secretly took two delegates and made his way to the Committee. Apparently they did not manage to get in, because nobody had time for them. When we got back to the plant during a break, we gathered together the second shift. In the presence of the Director himself, the work force categorically refused to take part in those negotiations. They said that the matter should be settled to the end through the Inter-factory Strike Committee. We are still with you! [...]

Lech Wałęsa:

[...] According to my calculations, 99% are on our side. That means we're winning by 99% and there we are. We still need just one percent. That one percent – all it needs is to stick it out!
[9]

Extract from the Appeal of the 64 Intellectuals (Warsaw):

Everyone - both the rulers and the ruled - must be driven by what is good for Poland. Under the present circumstances we should desist from arguments and from creating divisions within society by the use of thoughtless words and insulting epithets. There have been far too many slanderous campaigns of hatred within living memory. Let us learn to respect each other's dignity. [...] History will not forgive anyone, who would reach for a solution other than by the road to agreement. Let us, therefore, step onto that road, we appeal for consideration and for imagination, in the belief that, at this time, there is no more important matter for Poland.

Photo: Zbigniew Trybek

Photo: Zbigniew Trybek

Extract from a statement issued by the Inter-factory Strike Committee:

The first point in our demands is the key element. Without independent trade unions all other demands can be deleted in the future. This has happened many times in the short history of the Polish People's Republic. The official trade unions not only did not, and do not, stand in defence of our rights and interests but they demonstrate an even more negative attitude to our just strike action than do party and government circles. The severest criticism of our strike action came from Chairman Szydlak of the Central Board of Trade Unions [...] He described our strike as an indication of the presence of enemy forces and terrorism. His words carry a threat: "We will not give up our power, we will not share our power". [...] We have called on the government spokesman and will continue to call on him, to undertake negotiations. Delaying tactics are akin to cutting off one's own roots.

Extract from the minutes of a meeting of the Politburo of the Central Committee of the Polish United Workers Party:

Comrade Władysław Kruczek:

We are burdened with the responsibility for what we have already done and for the decisions, which we will take. One of our weaknesses is that we do not have the support of the Party behind us. Party members must be goaded into action, the real danger must be explained to them. [...] Let us call Comrade Pyka, give him help. We must defend the factories against the terrorist influence of KOR.

[...]

Comrade Wojciech Jaruzelski:

We must be mindful of Soviet interest, and take note of it. Our friends are very concerned by what is going on here. Movement of troops – both ours and our allies' – planned a long time ago – have been cancelled. We asked our allies to change the transportation route under the circumstances.

Comrade Edward Gierek:

[...] A psychosis of paralysis and fear caused by tension and hostility has evolved on a scale never before encountered. There is something in our society which has been growing for a number of years. There is a general crisis of confidence...

[...] I can undertake talks with the workers at any time. [1]

Extract from an article in "Głos Wybrzeża":

The abnormal situation in the Triple City has been going on for a long time now. The inhabitants of the city consider that the rhythm of public and personal life has been disrupted for far too long. Economic activity has become disorganised, and the private lives of the inhabitants made more difficult. People are unable to relax due to the state of nervous tension.

Extract from a report by the City Commander of the Civil Militia in Gdańsk:

Some sort of paranoia has evolved claiming that Gdańsk is surrounded by special commando units and tanks, which are waiting for an excuse to enter the city. Members of the Strike Committees appeal for the maintenance of order and ask that people desist from insulting officers of the Civil Militia and thereby do not give a pretext for intervention. [4]

Billboard slogan: United in our fraternal alliance, we fight in the cause of peace and socialism

General Krzysztoporski from the Ministry of the Interior in "An appraisal of the influence of organised anti-socialist group activities on the threat to the internal safety of the state":

[...] The methods adopted thus far in combating the activities of anti-socialist elements which break the rule of law, have not given the expected results. [...]

In view of the above, the following action is proposed:

– the initiation of decisive action in combating anti-socialist activities by introducing special measures in political and administrative spheres and with regard to law and order [...].

It should be stressed that we currently hold information concerning 43 people, mainly activists from organised anti-socialist groups, who should be investigated and put under temporary arrest. [2]

Extract from Ministry of the Interior information:

Central bodies of Church administration do not issue any information nor take up an official stance in the matter of the current situation. [...] The Diocesan Bishop of Gdańsk, Bishop Kaczmarek [...] considers that strike committees and anti-socialist groups are not partners of the Church and it is necessary to isolate the Church from their activities. [2]

Billboard slogan: All praise to those who are doing good work!

Photo: Bogusław Nicznalski

21-08-1980

Thursday

- *The Gdańsk Inter-factory Strike Committee now numbers 350 striking enterprises.*
- *Tadeusz Pyka is recalled and Deputy Prime Minister Mieczysław Jagielski heads the Government Commission, which continues to ignore the Inter-factory Strike Committee.*
- *A Government Commission headed by Kazimierz Barcikowski takes up negotiations with the strikers in Szczecin.*
- *Strike breaks out in the Lenin Steelworks in Kraków.*

From the Plenum of the Inter-factory Strike Committee:

— Ladies and gentlemen, I am from "Malmor". Yesterday information was leaked through here — in this room — that "Malmor" has betrayed the Inter-factory Strike Committee. That is not true. It is quite likely, but we don't know definitely, that talks with the government commission were undertaken by a delegation chosen by the management, something which is done quite often now in many factories in order to promote chaos and to cause as many enterprises to break away from the Inter-factory Strike Committee as possible. [...] I declare once again that we, the employees of "Malmor" have not given up and none of us will desert the Shipyard. [...]

Andrzej Kozicki:

I am a delegate from the Paris Commune Shipyard. I would like to pass on to all our colleagues here the information that, from the very start, our work-force has presented an unyielding attitude. Thanks to this attitude, so well supported by Andrzej Kołodziej, the chairman of our committee — at this moment at least 60–70% of the work-force is on a permanent sit-in strike. They take up positions on neat rows of benches, in front of the main gates, so that all passers-by can see that the Shipyard workers are, indeed, occupying the grounds of the Shipyard. [...] I believe that it is imperative at this stage to achieve maximum unity among all the people and to mass them in one place. Then nobody will be in a position to break down the solidarity within the working class and there will be no place for any provocation. [9]

Photo: Zbigniew Trybek

Strikers in the Gdynia Shipyard

Józef Kuczma (Shipyard in Gdynia):

On the other side of the gate there are thousands of people who have come here from the city, despite the bad weather. It is cold, there is a strong wind and it keeps raining. During Holy Mass we had something of a fright. At one point a helicopter appeared above us. It circled above us several times and then flew off, to return after a short while. It repeated this manoeuvre several times and finally dropped some leaflets but the strong wind carried them off some considerable distance, right up to the port canal. None of the leaflets fell on the Shipyard. After a moment the helicopter returns and once again drops some leaflets, this time from further away, but this time, again, without success. Once again they all fell into the canal. [...] We don't even know who was behind it, or what they hoped to achieve. [20]

Photo: Stanisław Składanowski

Lech Wałęsa:

I remember, I drew Olek Hall aside and told him: *"If there is an attack on the Shipyard, they're sure to get me, there'll be an accident or something like that – remember my wife and children, then"*. I was dreadfully tired, as were many people around me – psychologically at the end of their tether. It was then that the [Gdańsk] literary circle helped us to carry on. Led by Mr Będkowski. [...] We were in the Shipyard, stateless, in a free republic, where order was maintained by ourselves, identity existed in a state of suspension, but the future appeared grey and bleak. [...] Mr Będkowski was co-opted onto the Presidium of the Inter-factory Strike Committee to a standing ovation. [23]

Extract from a document of the Polish Independence League:

The ruling party stands to be judged by the very class from which it apparently takes its roots and in whose name it purports to rule. [...]
The striking shipyard workers and workers from other production enterprises in the Coastal Provinces who actively support them, do not constitute a threat either to Socialism or the safety of the Country. In the workshops which they occupy and which, on the strength of the Constitution of the Polish People's Republic, belong to them, the principles, ideals and laws the practice of which the government has long since departed, are at last being re-born. The unity of the nation is being recreated, a unity which puts an end to divisions and differences, together with a real sense of social integration and responsibility for the Country. [...]
The strikers are actively expressing what the entire Polish nation thinks and feels, and desires. Realisation of this should convince the authorities of the senselessness of using any form of force. Behind the strikers, stands the whole international trade union movement and an enormous majority of world opinion, which follows their peaceful, bloodless battle with bated breath – let us hope that it will be bloodless to the very end – knowing that it is not only the fate of Polish workers that is in the balance, but that of the whole of Poland and, indeed, the fate of Europe.

From a statement issued by the Inter-factory Strike Committee:

The Inter-factory Strike Committee, as representative of all enterprises, once again calls on the authorities to undertake talks with a view to fulfilling the demands made on the government commission, handed over in writing on 18th August to the Governor of Gdańsk, Professor Jerzy Kołodziejski. An open and democratically organised dialogue is the only means to end the strike. [...] The work-force of the Gdańsk Shipyard, whose territory has become the head-quarters of the Inter-factory Strike Committee, guarantees complete security for the government delegates while in its grounds for the duration of the talks.

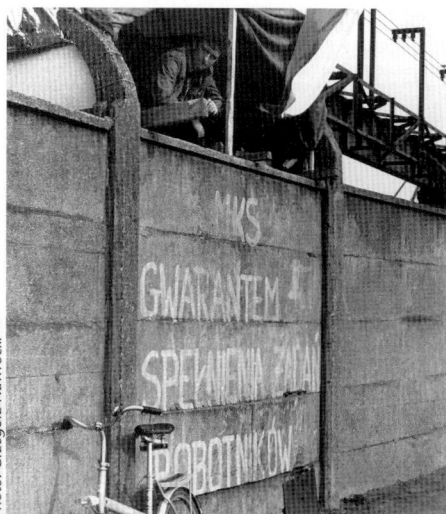

Photo: Grzegorz Nawrocki

Slogan on the wall: MKS (Inter-factory Strike Committee) – guarantor of fulfilment of demands

Extract from a meeting of the Provincial Headquarters in Gdańsk:

Comrade Jerzy Andrzejewski:

The Committee [Inter-factory Strike Committee] is working towards a moral and ideological change by such provocative means as misinformation, church masses etc. They have changed their organisational methods – some of the strikers take it in turns to visit family homes. Although the strike committees speak of it, the actual decision to end the strike lies with the Inter-factory Strike Committee, to which they are subject. The Repair Yard yesterday took a spontaneous decision to join the Inter-factory Strike Committee.

It has been established that "literature" is being transported from the Lenin Shipyard to the Paris Commune Shipyard by sea. KOR leaders are physically present in the Lenin Shipyard and they exhort and instruct the strikers.

[...] The Civil Militia is actively blocking the passage of information. [...] There are currently 1,200 militiamen in the Gdańsk, Gdynia and Sopot area. This force is sufficient. We have worked out suitable tactics for specific events and places. Today a vehicle carrying a large consignment of toothbrushes, toothpaste etc. to the Paris Commune Shipyard was intercepted.

[...] Officers of the Civil Militia are working towards the identification of members of the committee.   [3]

Extract from minutes of a meeting of the Politburo of the Central Committee of the Polish United Workers Party:

Comrade Stanisław Kania:

Gdańsk. The situation is still difficult. Since yesterday there has been some complication and escalation caused, among others, by the somewhat inept way the government commission has approached the talks. Two days ago two shipyards were in favour of opting out of the political demands and membership of the Inter-factory Strike Committee, today, however, they have declared they are joining it. And that is where our defeat lies. Comrade Pyka has been recalled from the commission; his place has been taken by Comrade Jagielski, who is leading the talks. [...]

Among the methods accepted by the team are:

– not undertaking talks with the Inter-factory Strike Committee, only with delegates from individual factories or enterprises,

– ensuring the avoidance of strikers taking to the streets,

– increasing discussions of Party activists with members, to explain the situation, warn of the dangers and consequences,

– the isolation, as far as is possible, of individual strike centres. [...]

Comrade Edward Gierek:

We must be prepared for the tense situation to continue for some time. That is why we must mobilise the Party, activate it, put into action all the consequences we are drawing from the situation. What we are faced with is symptoms of counter-revolution in the shape of the organised activity of terrorist groups who exert their influences on the working class.   [1]

Edward Gierek, 1st Secretary of the Polish United Workers Party

Extract from telexed information from the Provincial Committees to the Central Committee of the Polish United Workers Party:

Kraków:

The socio-political situation in the Lenin Steelworks plant. [...] The following problems were discussed during an open meeting of the Basal Party Organisation in the Machining Department (183 people took part):
– what is our government waiting for, it's time it took radical steps,
– trade unions are basically not fulfilling their role, as they concern themselves with only small matters such as, for instance, the organisation of funerals,
– why are there three newspapers in Kraków which have almost identical articles; is this not a waste of paper and could we not do with just one paper,
– the list of parliamentary candidates should be arranged alphabetically, and elections should not be conducted in the old undemocratic fashion – we now have the result of this form of government,
– as a statistical citizen I "eat" 72 kg of meat, I have a 5-member family, which means that we eat 360 kg of meat per year. That's incredible! Who does eat this meat?

Płock:

[...] Many of those taking part in the discussions [at Basal Party Organisation meetings] stressed that the Party must take stock and learn from the past. Lack of ties between the Party and individual work-forces has meant that the worker, insecure and lacking direction, has given his allegiance to those who have made him promises, regardless of the fact that those making the promises are anti-socialist elements.

Gorzów:

Some people are annoyed by the fact that we are spending too much time in treating the strikers with kid gloves and that the government should not bow to the demands of the Coastal Provinces.

It is proposed that names of the strike leaders should be published, together with their photographs and exhibited for the information of the public. After all, that is what the Western press and "[Radio] Free Europe" does. [1]

From a report by the Commander of the City Civil Militia in Gdańsk:

Large groups of troops and militia are stationed at the airport in Rembiechów and in the "Blue Beret" barracks, as well as on the military training grounds in Brętów [?], which have been relocated with the aim of putting down anti-socialist forces. A delegation from the Inter-factory Strike Committee arrived and stated that the strike in Gdańsk is just a simple workers' strike and does not have political overtones. [4]

Extract from minutes of a meeting of the Executive of the Gdańsk City Committee of the Polish United Workers Party:

RADMOR [?]: Things are being steered centrally. This is an organisation we know nothing about. Added to this there is a large group of well-concealed people. They come up with new arguments all the time. They come well prepared. This is not a spontaneous action. They are also active in other Provincial Cities. I believe we are losing Poland. [3]

Photo: Maciej Osiecki

Employee of the Mazowiecki House-Building Plant in Legionowo:

A Party meeting is due to start today at 9 o'clock. People who do not belong to the Party may also participate. [...] There are already some two hundred people in the hall. Now the Directors enter the hall, their Deputies, and Comrade Nader, the First Secretary of the Polish United Workers Party of the Plant and the Association. Next is the Secretary of the Legionów Town Committee of the Polish United Workers Party, Comrade Cybulski, and the clerk. [...] Comrade Nader is the first to speak. He reads from notes. [...] Suddenly he begins to improvise: *"It's all wrong, what do they hope to gain? It's against our interests, the interests of our Party. We must stand firm against the strikers".* [...] *"Are there any questions?"* – asks Comrade Nader pointedly. Silence reigns in the hall. Then, suddenly, Comrade Krawczuk, Chief Specialist, leaps up from his chair. He shouts: *"Comrades! What's the point of this meeting? We mustn't ape the strikers! Let's not waste time! Let us get back to work!".* At that a hostile murmur breaks out in the hall. A young man of about thirty gets up. He begins to speak. About the last congress of the Polish United Workers Party, about the promises made by Comrade Edward Gierek and not kept. How long must we wait for normal supplies of foodstuffs and meat on the home market? He speaks clearly and simply. Each one of us wanted to say the same. Each one of us felt the same deep down. But he was first. [...] There is a burst of applause, loud clapping, the atmosphere is charged with support for the speaker. A second participant stands up, then a third. They shout: *"We don't want to eat brawn, black puddings and patés made from toilet paper!".* A feeling of emotion takes over the hall. This Party meeting turns into a demonstration of solidarity with the strikers.

[...]

Comrade Cybulski asks to be heard. He starts with fine words: *"Poland, our Fatherland, it is our duty to take responsibility for time wasted".* [...] Someone shouts: *"Where's the sugar? Where's the meat and meat products to feed my family and myself?".* [...]

Tempers in the hall rise. A young man gets up abruptly. He asks whether his stomach is any different to that of a militiaman. Why does the militiaman earn 14 thousand and he does not? Is his child any different from the child of the militiaman? Why does the militiaman get an allowance of 700 zloties for the first child, and he only gets 100, then 500 for the second child and he only 70? Are they a chosen people?

[...] *"Where is the statue to commemorate the Gdańsk Shipyard victims of 1970?"* – people shout. I steal a glance at the main table. Comrade Cybulski sits, his face in his hands. Nader, like a fish out of water, tries to get a word in. The clerk, her head bent, pretends to be busy writing down what is said.

[...] At last Comrade Nader once again speaks: *"Everything we have heard here, Comrades, will be put down in the minutes and will be presented to the Central Committee. And now I propose we conclude our meeting".*

[...] The participants remain by themselves. Now, at this moment, we need someone who would stand up and say: *"We'll stay here until our common matters, our concerns and our problems are resolved".* I believe that one such voice would unite everybody. Unfortunately there was no such voice. [...] Slowly, with a feeling of disappointment, people leave the hall in small groups. [9]

Photo: Zbigniew Trybek

22-08-1980

Friday

- *Second round of talks between the Szczecin Inter-factory Strike Committee and the Government Commission.*
- *Strikes break out in Kraków and Skawina.*
- *In the evening a delegation of the Inter-factory Strike Committee meets in Gdańsk with Deputy Prime Minister Jagielski.*

Paweł (Gdynia Shipyard Independent Printing Works):

During the night an attack was prepared. They brought in ZOMO units [Mechanised Riot Troops of the Civil Militia] from Golędzinów to Gdynia and tried to attack the printing works. The action was called „Operation Wieczorek". This is all information gathered from taps on radio communications; we tap their radio communications vehicles. [...] The operation was called off when they saw that we were prepared to defend ourselves. [7]

Blockaded entry to the port in Gdynia

Photo: Zbigniew Trybek, State Archives in Gdańsk

Photo: Mirosław Stepniak

Stanisław Wądołowski (Shipyard in Szczecin):

People took rosters, talked, read books aloud, every hour they listened to the news, ate and slept. We were in constant dread that they might attack us and everybody was worried when there was no fresh news. Relatives waited outside the gates, sometimes you could get a pass out of the Shipyard. To an independent observer it probably looked like a gigantic picnic for 10 thousand people when the weather is not too good, there is nowhere to go and you are busy doing everything and nothing. [36]

Letter from a single mother (signed by other mothers working in the Railroad Hospital in Gdańsk):

I am the mother of a 13-year old son. On behalf of all single mothers in Poland I would like to present our demands to the authorities of the Polish People's Republic.

We, the mothers of the Polish People's Republic, ask for an increase in family benefits, in line with those which employees of the Ministry of the Interior and the Polish Army receive. [...]

Are our children's stomachs more resistant to black pudding, brawn and cheese and would they not like to eat the occasional piece of meat – these are, after all, children and their bodies need more sustenance.

Jacek Kuroń:

[20th August, Warsaw] They carried out a thorough search, which lasted a long time. In the course of it, they stopped everyone who came in. It was a planned trap. They only let out Western journalists, who were confused and did not quite know what was going on. They kept on at me to give them information, statements, interviews. They were thrown out but kept coming back. [...] I was taken to Grenadierów Street, to the militia station.

[...] The 48 hours [of detention] were over. I was in a state. Would they charge me, or would I be let out? Release! I go out, I'm weak at the knees with joy, because I have so much to do now. Two security policemen approached me. „Master Jacek, we can give you a lift."

They did give me a lift – to the militia station in Żoliborz. Another 48 hours. [14]

Lech Wałęsa (during plenary discussions of the Inter-factory Strike Committee):

[...] I wish to state formally that if the authorities keep on arresting members of KOR and of other socio-political organisation, there will not be any negotiations. They pulled the wool over our eyes, they are still doing it and they want to carry on doing it! We have been waiting over a week for them to come [...]. They can't arrest and detain people who don't lead us – since we lead ourselves, they just help us now as they did before. They have opened some people's eyes – about history and about what is owing to us.

[...] The people here, from "Elektromontaż" and from other shipyards who distributed our leaflets well, apparently about twenty of them are in jail. And that is why I appeal to the authorities: I want to see them here! [9]

Tadeusz Mazowiecki:

Some of the signatories of the *Appeal of Intellectuals* had an idea that, perhaps, this appeal is too little, that we should actually go there, and show our solidarity with the strikers by our presence among them. [...] We went to Gdańsk with Professor Geremek. In the evening we arrived at the gate to the Shipyard and asked to see Mr Lech Wałęsa, or any other member of the Executive of the Inter-factory Strike Committee. We were taken to the plenary negotiations room (there were almost permanent discussion sessions). It turned out that we had arrived just as there the first glimmer of hope appeared for the start of talks between the government commission and the Inter-factory Strike Committee.

Lech Wałęsa:

I asked concretely, what they had to offer us because we were really in need of help. To which Geremek answered: *"We're intellectuals. We don't fit in but we can take on an advisory role, as specialist"*. Now, there was an idea! The missing link had turned up on its own. [...] There wasn't time to check the references of our experts. My question: *"How long will you stay*

here with us?"*, Mazowiecki answered: *"To the end"*. They had come just in time. The 21 demands were excellent but in negotiations and then in practice they could well be torn to shreds. [...] This was a bridging link, which was also handy for the authorities. They were probably concerned – and rightly so – by the possible radicalism of expression of nervous, poorly educated people. [23]

Extract from confidential notes made by the Inter-factory Strike Committee's team of experts, concerning talks with the Government Commission:

Notes concerning possible compromises in the negotiations (according to numeration of demands):

1. As regards the name of the unions, the emotive "free" can be dropped and "independent" substituted in its place, to be understood as independent of employers, the remaining criteria in accordance with statutory law and regulations guaranteeing the freedom and independence of union organisations.

[...]

3. [...] guarantees of freedom of speech and publication apply to the liberalisation of censorship, the legalisation of independent publications, the scope of which is to be agreed with the authorities and with the guarantee that mass media sources will be available to representatives of various faiths (v. important – no compromise here). [8]

Tadeusz Mazowiecki in the Health & Safety room, Gdańsk Shipyard

Photo: Bogusław Nieznalski

From minutes of a meeting of the Politburo of the Central Committee of the Polish United Workers Party:

Comrade Stanisław Kania:

The situation continues to evolve in an unsatisfactory manner. [...] Gdańsk – the situation is intensifying, there is a growing determination [...]. Szczecin – talks continue but the strikers have a single-minded and determined attitude. The majority of members of the strike committees are Party members. There is considerable determi-nation in the demands made. [...] A new aspect is the Appeal of the Intellectuals (with 64 signatories), who do not place themselves on our side although they do not appear to be anti-socialist and therefore it is difficult to class them as one. [...]

Comrade Edward Babiuch:

Time is not on our side. The situation is deteriorating. [...] We are dealing with a crisis of confidence on the part of the public towards the authorities. The enemy is attacking the Party, and the activists complain. Under the circumstances this is not a time for sentiments and friendships. A crucial matter for the Party and for the country. It is high time that we all upheld the authority of Comrade Edward Gierek, which has recently been undermined. There is still considerable respect in the Party and in society for this authority. [...]

Two days ago, I presented the First Secretary of the Central Committee with my resignation from the position of Prime Minister. I personally believe that if we regroup on a larger scale, then we will achieve a better credibility. Wherever there is a crisis in the world, the head of government changes. [...] The decision, which I have taken, was made following my stay in Szczecin.

Comrade Edward Gierek:

I am not putting forward my resignation, although my authority has considerably diminished. [...] Complaints are laid at my door, too. But I will not tender my resignation, unless the Central Committee demands it of me and then I will not fight it. It was with due humility that I accepted the position of First Secretary and with due humility I will accept my dismissal; but I will do so under normal circumstances and not in the wake of conflicts, because that would leave a long-lasting scar on the credibility of the Party, of which I have been a member for almost 50 years. [...]

We do not have much time. At this time, we are faced with, above all, a political defeat. [...] Nothing of today's meeting must be allowed to leave this room (particularly mention of Comrade Brezhniev's letter; a rumour is already rife that I was in Moscow yesterday). The plenary meeting should be called for Sunday 24th August.   [24]

Extract from a telex from the Secretary's Office of the Gdańsk Provincial Committee of the Polish United Workers Party and Ja Łabęcki, member of the Central Committee of the Polish United Workers Party to Stanisław Kania:

In accordance with our conversation I am forwa ding our stance on the question whether the gover ment commission should, or should not, underta talks with the Inter-factory Strike Committee.

We consider that these talks should be undertake Reasons: [...]

3. Society feels that this is the quickest and mo effective way to resolve the conflict.

4. A deciding factor in bringing the situation ba to normal is to achieve an understanding as quick as possible:
– time is on their side, because it gives the a chance to strengthen themselves both organisati nally and ideologically (the clergy),
– there is danger of the country being affected,
– the strikers are being joined by intellectual cir les, and by cultural/creative circles, and this will b come even more aggravated once young people sta their terms at high schools and universities.
[...]

11. Irresponsible decisions, taken in the first sta of the talks (particularly the decisions made duri the night), caused a breakdown in confidence in t credibility of the decisions made by the Governme Commission and this is now causing problems in t commission's current endeavours.

Photo: Romuald Broniarek

Extract from a cryptogram from the Head of Staff, Deputy Provincial Commander of the Civil Militia in Gdańsk:

In view of the socio-political situation which has evolved in the Coastal Provinces, it has been confirmed that employees of "RADMOR" and "MORS" are carrying out systematic taps on conversations between those members of the Civil Militia who have cause to use radio-telephones.

In view of this, I suggest as follows:

– not to pass on information which, in view of the nature of our activities and aims is of a confidential nature,

– to restrict conversations to an absolute minimum until such time as special codes are issued. [4]

Extract from information from the Gdańsk Provincial Command of the Civil Militia to the Ministry of the Interior:

We have received information indicating increased interest in the situation in the Triple City by Chinese employees of "Chipolbrok", who live in the "Chinese House" in Gdynia. In recent days they have all been equipped with photographic cameras, which they did not have previously. The object of their interest appears to be mainly the work-places which are on strike and where they take photographs.

[...] A decidedly negative speech has been reported, made by the priest, Father J. Balicki, who said a Mass for some 500 children from classes VII and VIII. In his sermon, he told them, among others: *"The great majority of our parishioners are shipyard workers*

[...]. *We are familiar with their problems and we consider that they are right in striking. Indeed, how can they not strike, when there is no freedom in our country"*. [4]

Extracts from telexes from the Provincial Committee to the Central Committee of the Polish United Workers Party:

Tarnów:

It has been noted that a frequent subject brought up in discussions among Party circles concerns the quality of Party ranks in the context of the Coastal Provinces: "There are so many of us and so what?".

Gdańsk:

Strike leaders are avoiding hostile activities. Yesterday, for instance, they released the Director of the Paris Commune Shipyard and allowed him to leave.

Katowice:

Yesterday we noted a marked influx of people from the Coastal Provinces, who try to ferment the fears of local people. This is notable in the increased distribution of leaflets carrying hostile messages, which contain exhortations to solidarity with the strikers. [...] These attempt were met with immediate rejection by the people, and particularly by Party members.

[...] An example, which illustrates the attempt to influence people in our Province, is the statement made by Roman Marian, a fitter from the "Cedler" Steelworks: "I came back from Gdynia yesterday. I am shocked by what I saw there – the port is dead, normal life in the city has stopped. A certain trawler owner, who has a villa and is very well off, tried to persuade me to go on strike, too, when I return to Sosnowiec". [...]

Since attempts to ferment fears locally have not been successful, they have tried to find new ways to deprecate [!] our region, sending postcards to the Central Committee with KOR demands. A postcard was sent from Tychy carrying the message: "We demand true information in the press, democratic elections, all Saturdays to be free of work (that must surely be possible)".

Ostrołęka:

During discussion, our Party activists, from both town and country, posed many questions which were tinged with a good dose of bitterness [...] Active Party members are reluctant to take part in organising meetings, as they meet with accusations of joint culpability in allowing the present situation to develop. [1]

Photo: Zenon Mirota

Slogans on the Shipyard walls: "The strike goes on"; "Victory only through solidarity and patience"; "Long live free and independent trade unions and world-wide peace"; "Justice and equality for all the nation"

Photo: Stefan Kraszewski/ADM/PAP

23-08-1980

Saturday

- In the Gdańsk Shipyard the first edition of the "Solidarność Strike Information Bulletin" appears.
- In the evening, talks between the Gdańsk Inter-factory Strike Committee and the Government Commission begin, they are transmitted on the radio-transmitter system throughout the Shipyard.
- In Szczecin talks between the strikers and Barcikowski's commission continue.

Extract from an Inter-factory Strike Committee Statement (in the "Solidarność Strike Information Bulletin"):

We wish to point out that the false representation of the situation in the Coastal Provinces and of the intentions of the striking workers strikes at the remainders of credibility which censored newspapers, radio and television may still have and does nothing to calm the tempers of the public. We demand that all Poles are given full and true information concerning our demands.

Extract from the Inter-factory Strike Committee's meeting:

Tadeusz Mazowiecki:

[...] Having come here, we are now convinced of your extreme common-sense. [...] We will try to help you, but the role of the experts must be confined to advice, while decisions lie in the hands of the Presidium. [...]

Lech Wałęsa:

That's all very well, but let us remember one thing. To this point we have been prepared and – really – you could say that we were winning, but now, we are not too well prepared for this next stage. That is why I propose that you make yourselves comfortable, have a rest, go for a walk, and we – as the Plenum – will get ready for the next round. [9]

Zbigniew Lis (Gdańsk Shipyard):

Throughout the entire strike I did not leave the Shipyard premises once – with a single exception. As chief of security I had to fetch the government delegation. This consisted, among other, of Jagielski, Kołodziejski, Fiszbach. We had to sign an undertaking that we would not allow anyone to come closer to them than one metre and that would guarantee their safety. Everything happened so fast. Today, I believe that it was very risky on our part, after all there may have been a provocateur in the crowd, who could have attacked them.

[...] Nobody touched them, but it would not have taken much for the shipyard workers to have lynched us – the security team – for being too rough in preventing cameramen from an American television team who were pushing us. The strikers shouted: *"Let them through, it's a free press"*. [30]

Photo: Zbigniew Trybek

Waiting for the arrival of the Government Commission

Lech Wałęsa and Mieczysław Jagielski

Mieczysław Jagielski:

When I made my way to Gdańsk, nobody told me to what extent I was empowered. I heard only: *"Go and sort out this social conflict. And make it quick because the situation is very serious"*.

[...] I remember my first arrival, hostile shouts, thumping on the sides of the bus we arrived in. [...] I felt the hostility. It was horrendous. There I was, with a serious heart condition, and I had to represent the authorities with due dignity. [28]

Lech Wałęsa:

Together with Director Gniech and several members of the Inter-factory Strike Committee, I make my way from the Safety and Hygiene room down a narrow path between crowds of shipyard workers. Jagielski gets out of the coach. His face is pale and drawn. He has a black briefcase under his arm, Fiszbach and the rest of them follow after him. I go up to him, extend my hand and welcome him to the Shipyard. I am relaxed, smiling. *"Leszek! Leszek!"* the crowd chants with one voice. It is intended to express a vote of confidence which the strikers have given us, the visitors are meant to take note of it, to realise how far our mandate goes. A forest of people, arms raised with clenched fists. [23]

Genowefa Klamann (Gdańsk Shipyard):

We women, gathered together in the right hand corner of the room near the door wielded our knives since early morning, cutting bread, sausage, making sandwiches, to ensure that all those who made their way to that corner, after a short, intensive night, would have something to eat. Every day, special teams brought us supplies of cucumbers, tomatoes, peppers, butter, bread. [...] There was one day when all they brought was a bath-tub full of black pudding, which we tried to divide up fairly, so that everyone got at least a piece.

[...] At the moment when the government delegation first entered the room with Mr Jagielski at its head, we women were paralysed and just stood there, knives in our hands, not taking our eyes off the entrance, where the atmosphere was so charged and so extra-ordinary. The room was brightly lit, it was quiet, there was an atmosphere of con-centration, and we melted in with the expectant crowd. [20]

Grzegorz Nawrocki:

In a corner of the room, the ladies are making sandwiches. The delegate from "Fermstal" observes that the ones being made for the people who are to talk in the smaller room are a little better. The sandwich lady protests, saying that she only had one tin of "Baltona" [ham]. *"That's what we're fighting for"* shouts the delegate from "Fermstal" – *"and not for them to get better food. Let them taste what the workers have to eat. Are their stomachs any different?"*

The sandwich lady promises that, in future, they will all be the same.

And then Wałęsa says into the microphone: *"We welcome the delegation"*. [7]

Extract from discussions between the Government Commission and the Inter-factory Strike Committee:

Lech Wałęsa:

The telephones are not working. [...] Can I please know why they are being blocked? [...]

Lech Bądkowski:

[...] The governor announced that, as far as I remember, as of 11.30 communication with Szczecin had been restored. However, as regards our demand that telephone communication with Warsaw be restored, the governor answered that he had to check whether this demand was considered impossible.

Zbigniew Zieliński (member of the Government Commission):

Well, you see, last night there was a hurricane over Warsaw, which caused havoc in many parts of the city. I was there. [...]

Alina Pienkowska:

I would like you to know that telephone communication with Warsaw was blocked on Friday, a week ago. There was no mention of a hurricane then.
[...]

Andrzej Gwiazda:

[...] It's basically a simple matter, all it takes is one command.

Lech Wałęsa:

Seeing that there are difficulties, perhaps we shouldn't discuss anything, let's just listen to what the Prime Minister and the rest of the government have to say to our demands.
[...]

Mieczysław Jagielski:

Mr Chairman, ladies and gentlemen. I have tried to make a brief resume, as far as is possible, of our points of view on each of the matters which have been put before us. [...] I, too, want to be honest and I want to be able – here, in Gdańsk and everywhere else, too – to look people in the eye. [...] If I were to undertake something which was to be unrealistic that would simply mean that I was not being honest with you.

Lech Wałęsa:

Thank you Mr Prime Minister, we have listened carefully to what you have said. However, I don't think we've established why it is that every so often this happens – this time it has been ten years and I suspect that another ten will pass and we will return to the same point at which we are now. [...] We have not heard, here, why it is that this happens, why we keep returning, running round in circles, nor what guarantees we, as workers, have. [...] I believe that something is not quite right in the way things are steered, the way they run, the testing they undergo. I'm just a worker but that is how I see it.

Mieczysław Jagielski:

[...] I agree. Something is not quite right. I propose the following, let us come to an agreement, then trust me: I will put the matter to the next Plenum of the Central Committee.

Lech Wałęsa:

Let us point you in the right direction. One solution is most surely what we have proposed: free trade unions, strong and active, the way working world would like to see. This is not a matter of politics. It's really a matter of counter-balance and control. We will control ourselves, we will see our own mistakes, propose our own solutions but never the way it is done now, by making things more difficult for people who want to say something, do something, by arrests, detainment and the expansion of the machinery of power, in other words the militia. Because if everything is in order, the government is in order, then it will not have to surround itself with militia and the Police Security. [9]

Photo: Bogusław Nieznalski

Model of monument to commemorate victims of December 70 (design: Bogdan Pietruszka of the Gdańsk Shipyard)

Extract from minutes of meeting
of the Politburo of the Central Committee
of the Polish United Workers Party:

Comrade Kania:

The strike situation has not changed. There is a certain relaxation of tension in the Coastal Provinces. Following consultation with Comrades Jagielski and Zieliński, we have decided to undertake talks with the Inter-factory Strike Committee, although this is obviously to their advantage. [...] The Inter-factory Strike Committee has demanded that communication links with Szczecin and the rest of the country be made available. We agreed to Szczecin, but the country – no. [...]

Comrade Gierek:

You know the situation. We do not need to go into it. We need time to consider the text of the speech for the Plenum because Monday could well be a disaster. The "to be or not to be" of socialism is at stake. Each one of us present here must put himself at the disposal of the Party. [...]

Comrade Kania:

Reality indicates that the country is headed for catastrophe. We put great store by the Plenum, but there are fears, too, because if that does not make any changes, then what is left? Force? – no!   [24]

Edward Gierek:

Borys Aristov, the Soviet Ambassador has been in almost daily contact with me. He shared his fears with me and expressed anxiety about the future of socialism in Poland. Before the IV Plenum he telephoned me on Brezhniev's direct line and told me: "If things are going against you then put the boot in, we'll help".   [12]

Leonid Brezhniev and Edward Gierek

Extract from telexes from Provincial Committees to the Central Committee of the Polish United Workers Party:

Kraków:

At 13.25 a group of 200 employees of the steel workshop (No. 2 gang) at the Lenin Steelworks put together demands addressed to the government of the Polish People's Republic, the Management of the Lenin Steelworks and the management of the workshop.

The text of the demands follows: [...]

– introduce a free and uncensored press,

– stop the armaments race, space race, the cold war and meteorological warfare, and use the money to develop agriculture and river regulation,

– curtail exports to the USSR and reduce the number of Russian troops stationed on Polish territory by 50 percent,

– halt aid to developing countries,

– we also demand that the government of the Polish People's Republic take political steps to ensure that the eastern territories, which were Polish lands before 1939, are returned to the Motherland,

– we demand friendship and co-operation with all nations worldwide,

– an end to Party dictatorship.

Szczecin:

A student of the University of Wrocław presented himself at the port in Świnoujście, wanting to manifest his solidarity with the strikers. He was passed on to the Civil Militia.

Leszno:

Yesterday two goods trains, one from a westerly direction, one from the south, arrived at Leszno station covered in slogans hostile to the Party and the USSR. This graffiti was removed. In the town of Boszkowo a hostile slogan was found painted on the road and this was removed. Editors of "Słowo Powszechne" were distributed a list of the political demands made by the striking workers of the Coastal Provinces. The names of the editors have been established. [1]

Photo: Jerzy Szot

From Ministry of the Interior information:

Bishop Kaczmarek issued a proclamation which will be read out at all masses in the Diocese of Gdańsk. In it he states: "I trust that you are all sensible and must surely be aware that to continue the strike and to draw it out indefinitely does not have a positive effect on your families or your own interests, nor that of society in general, in fact – quite the reverse – it serves only to deepen the crisis and the atmosphere of tension among your families and the entire Coastal Provinces". [2]

24-08-1980

Sunday

- *Talks with the Government Commission are no longer continued, either in Gdańsk, or Szczecin.*
- *The IV Plenum of the Central Committee of the Polish United Workers Party takes place; there are changes in the government – Józef Pińkowski takes over the office of Prime Minister; Edward Gierek's final public appearance.*

STRAJK SOLIDARNOŚCI TRWA NADAL.

Photo: Grzegorz Nawrocki

Solidarity strike still on

Extract from a conversation between Lech Wałęsa and foreign and home journalists:

"Is the point which you are fighting for not a matter of high politics?"

"No, we want to be the hosts in our places of work, at our work-stations – that is not politics, this is the 21 points."

"Where did you personally pick up the language of politics?"

"I learnt it from the blood of 1970."

[11]

Władysław Szymanek (Szczecin):

On the first Sunday of the strike, two beautiful rainbows appeared over the Shipyard, this brought us some comfort because – as people say – it is a portent of hope, it heralds victory. [21]

Aleksander Tuerner (economic technician, at the Chemical works in the town of Police):

Everybody makes for the television to see the news. In Warsaw, the Plenum has taken place – there's a new Prime Minister, new Secretaries. But the top man still stands there and talks. There is disappointment and anger. We were almost sure that after all that has happened we would never see that gentleman on television again. And yet, there you are! [20]

Photo: Jan Kups

Photo: Jan Kups

From minutes of a meeting of the Politburo of the Central Committee of the Polish United Workers Party:

Comrade Mieczysław Jagielski
(arrived at the meeting straight from Gdańsk):

The strike in Gdańsk is led by a group of thinking people, directed from Warsaw. Their strategy is to draw the strike out at all costs and win. Political problems are dominant. They have influenced and threatened the work force with whom we could have reached an agreement. Wałęsa has advisors, his staff has experts from various disciplines and professions, I saw people there who are well known to me. [...] They have a selected, trained and disciplined team which orchestrates people's reactions to our speeches. Lack of communication with Warsaw is a very sore point. [...] They delayed the opening of the talks in order to lay the blame on the Government Commission.

In front of the Shipyard gates there is a huge aggressive crowd. Mainly young people, the older ones are calmer. Everyone makes the "victory" sign with two fingers. They make a show of cheering Leszek (Wałęsa). We are met with hostile shouts. [...]

While I was speaking, I was rudely interrupted, but by the end I had managed to put forward our stance and for three hours answered their questions. [...] It is difficult to conduct these talks, we are belittled, humiliated. [...] How long do they intend to strike? – I don't know. The crowd in front of the gates is getting larger all the time.   [1]

Extract from a speech made by Tadeusz Fiszbach at the IV Plenum of the Central Committee of the Polish United Workers Party (published in the "Głos Wybrzeża"):

It must be said openly that the content, form and language of our dialogue with society was, all too frequently, at cross purposes with society's views, all too frequently it appeared to be a statement of our aims rather than a mirror of the thoughts, needs and problems of working people and, in particular, of the working classes.

[...] It would be a mistake to judge that the strike in the Gdańsk Shipyard and subsequently in several hundred other places of work in the Triple City was the result of the activities of a limited group of representatives of anti-socialist forces, or that its inception, course and aims grew from a background alien to the working class or hostile to People's Poland. [...]   [8]

Photo: Stanisław Jakubowski/ADM/PAP

Slogan on banner: Hard work and community activities multiply the strength of the Polish People's Republic

From a speech by Jan Łabęcki, First Secretary of the Basal Party Organisation in the Gdańsk Shipyard
(shorthand notes from Plenum discussions):

I would make so bold as to say: the Party should make an effort to throw off the muck it is carrying. It is high time to take this step, irrespectively of position held or rung of the ladder. Only work counts, not fine words. Everyone should be held responsible for the work he does and the effects it brings. These are the demands of the workers in the Shipyard, and have been for some time now – from the pre-congress campaign, from the post-congress explanatory campaign and at this moment from the strike committees. These are, after all, our own slogans – we must not now allow them to be stolen by the dissidents. We must legalise certain deserving matters and make them public. We cannot go forward in our current tone and in darkness. I'm sorry if the style of this is not quite

Extract from Edward Gierek's speech at the IV Plenum of the Central Committee of the Polish United Workers Party:

I listened to the speeches of our Comrades from the Coastal Provinces with heightened emotion. They are imbued with a variety of truths which, to me, a seasoned worker and activist, have a particularly strong appeal.   [8]

Edward Gierek (at a meeting with the Secretaries of the Provincial Committees following the IV Plenum):

I would ardently like to ask everyone for one thing: that – immediately, although today you will not have time yet, but first thing tomorrow morning – that you begin to develop a Party offensive, we must start to act now, we must attack, irrespective of how the comrades view today's plenary meeting.

[...] It could be that we were a little too free with our money, that not everything was calculated the way it should have been, and then perhaps – indeed, more than likely – that some of the things we built need not have been built [...] But, Comrades, it is also a fact that what we did build and what we may yet build with what we still have on stock – will last Poland for another 15 years! That's what we should talk about!

[...] If we speak only of how bad we were, how bad we are and what we have done wrong, then, Comrades, we ourselves will begin to believe that we are not worth anything. [...] And that is what, in all sincerity, I would ask you to do – slowly, sensibly but resolutely emerge from that atmosphere of apathy, that lack of confidence which is specific in that it spreads and infects ever greater numbers of people.

[...] I know how hard things are for you but, Comrades, we do not have it easy here either – believe us. [...] Some of that feeling of tension was responsible for Comrade Babiuch's decision to resign from Party leadership and from the government. [...] That decision had some influence in the streets; it, too, caused not a little tension and gave rise to the opinion that Poland is leaderless. But I believe that, once Comrade Babiuch has had a chance to rest then, after some thought, he will come to himself and we'll try to make him a place as he deserves.   [1]

Photo: Tadeusz Zagoździński/ADM/PAP

From left: Edward Gierek, Henryk Jabłoński during the IV Plenum of the Central Committee of the Polish United Workers Party

Extract from telex information from the Gdańsk Provincial Committee to the Central Committee of the Polish United Workers Party:

Political endeavours aimed at calming the situation are becoming increasingly difficult as within society, and this includes Party members, solidarity sympathies are becoming ever more frequent. [...] E.g. in the Gdańsk Pruszcz area some of the Party members have taken positions on the strike committees. [1]

Extract from Ministry of the Interior information:

In accordance with current undertakings 20 people have been detained pending enquiries, 7 of whom were detained for the third time (incl. among others, Jacek Kuroń). The Civil Militia forces are carrying out intensive action throughout the country, particularly in the areas where conflict is rife.

E.g. in Gdańsk, 60 taxi-drivers had their licences revoked in the last few days, for helping the Inter-factory Strike Committee. [2]

Extract from information from the Provincial Headquarters of the Civil Militia to the Ministry of the Interior:

People staying in the Triple City for the Intervision Festival in Sopot have expressed concern not only at the situation in the Triple City, but at the prospect of intervention by the Soviet Union. As an example, a member of the Portuguese team enquired of their guide several times whether it is true that units of the Soviet Army are stationed around Gdańsk, with orders to intervene in the place of units of the Civil Militia and Security Police, or the Polish Army.

[...] Father Hilary Jastak has made his customary negative speeches. He even went so far as to make provocative statements that, in December 1970, workers were shot at and that it could still come to this now. [4]

Pope John Paul II in a proclamation to the Primate of Poland, Cardinal Wyszyński, published in the "Solidarność Strike Information Bulletin":

I pray that the Polish Episcopy, led by its Primate, and helped by Our Lady who is the defender of our Nation, can once again help the Nation in its hard fight for its daily bread, for social justice and for guarantees of its natural rights to its own life and development.

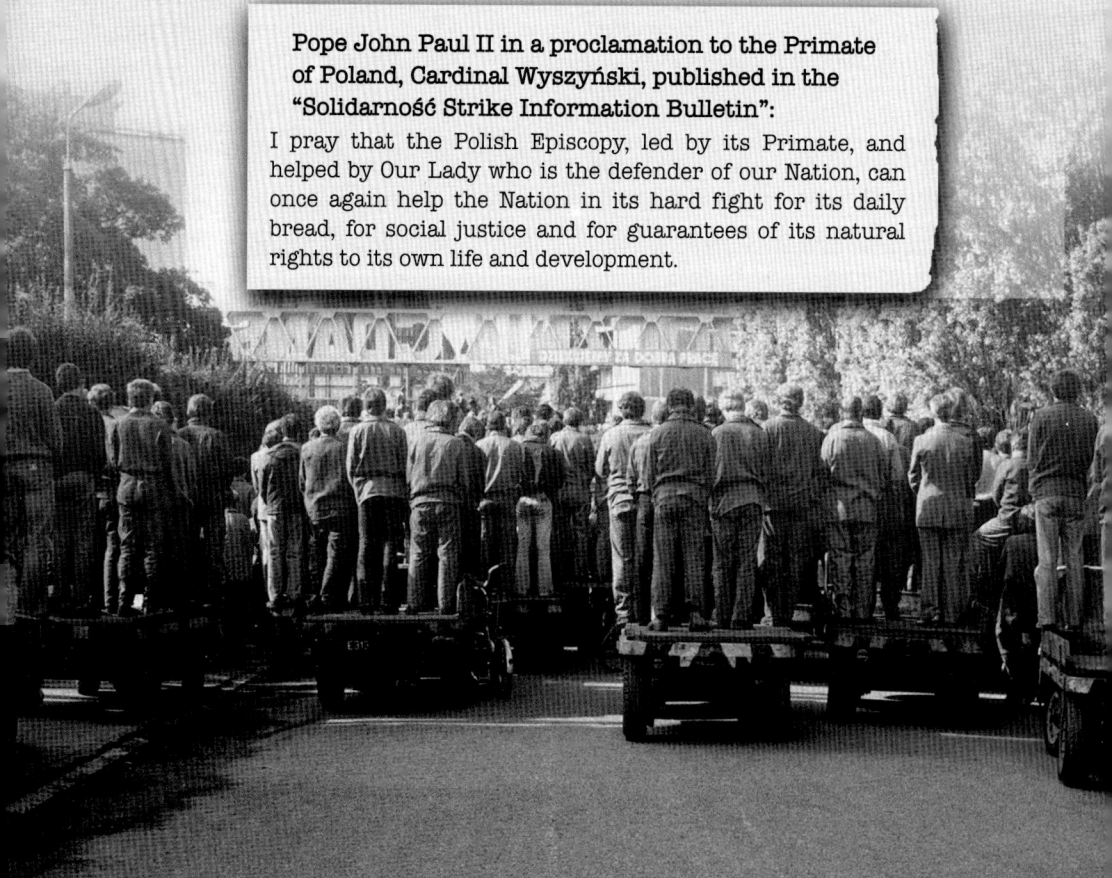

Photo: Zbigniew Trybek

Fot. Stanisław Składanowski

25-08-1980

poniedziałek

- *W Szczecinie strajkują 142 zakłady; odbywa się kolejna tura rozmów z Komisją Rządową.*
- *„Wieczór Wybrzeża" jako pierwsza oficjalna gazeta informuje o istnieniu gdańskiego MKS i 21 postulatów.*
- *W trakcie wieczornych rozmów z MKS wojewoda Jerzy Kołodziejski zobowiązuje się do odblokowania łączności telefonicznej z resztą kraju.*
- *Biuro Polityczne KPZR powołuje specjalną Komisję ds. Polski pod kierunkiem Michaiła Susłowa.*

Protest I zastępcy dyrektora Stoczni im. Komuny Paryskiej wobec Komitetu Strajkowego, Gdynia:

Niniejszym zgłaszam oficjalny protest przeciwko zagarnięciu na polecenie Komitetu Strajkowego 24 sierpnia o godzinie 21.50 większej ilości papieru z pomieszczeń traserni okrętowej. Papier ten jest niezbędny dla wykonywania dokumentacji kadłubowej. [...]

Z odpowiedzi Komitetu Strajkowego:

informujemy, że ów „zagarnięty" papier niezbędny jest dla prawidłowego funkcjonowania Wolnej Drukarni Stoczni Gdynia.

Praca Wolnej Drukarni służy przede wszystkim rzetelnemu informowaniu społeczeństwa o rozwoju sytuacji strajkowej, co wydaje nam się w chwili obecnej sprawą najważniejszą, tym bardziej że dziennikarze pism oficjalnych nie otrzymują najprawdopodobniej rzetelnych wiadomości i prasa partyjna roi się od najróżniejszych kalumnii wypaczających sytuację na Wybrzeżu.   [8]

Z reportażu z Wolnej Drukarni Stoczni Gdynia w „Biuletynie Informacyjnym":

Chociaż już wiadomo z opowiadań, że to prawdziwa drukarnia, wrażenie jest piorunujące. Za zakratowanymi drzwiami, przez które warta przepuszcza nas pojedynczo, jest kilka pomieszczeń. [...] Przy maszynach kręcą się ludzie w kombinezonach, odkładają zadrukowane partie, podkładają papier, otrzepują ryzy. Na końcu, w osobnym pokoju, jest mnóstwo kaset z czcionkami. Przy wejściu wielki stół ze starannie poukładanymi biuletynami strajkowymi. Ich jakość jest imponująca – wyraźne, doskonale czytelne, niepodobne do bibuły, do której jesteśmy przyzwyczajeni.

[...] Andrzej Butkiewicz (szef drukarni):
– Na dobę robimy jakieś 60–80 tysięcy.
[...]
– Dla kogo jest przeznaczone to, co drukujecie?
Paweł [pracownik drukarni]: Głównie dla MKS. Przywożę z Gdańska teksty MKS-u do drukowania i większość gotowej produkcji wraca potem do Gdańska. Część idzie na potrzeby Stoczni w Gdyni albo na miasto i dalej.
[...] Jeszcze żadna większa przesyłka nie wpadła. Najpierw wywoziliśmy samochodami, ale od czasu, jak zaczęli je zatrzymywać [milicja], przeszliśmy na koncepcję małych paczek. Mnóstwo ludzi idzie, wynoszą małe

Fot. Zbigniew Trybek

Niezależna drukarnia w Stoczni Gdańskiej

paczki – i docierają prawie wszystkie, no chyba tylko oprócz tych, które rozdrapią ludzie po drodze. [...] Dzisiaj na przykład wysłałem taką paczkę do Wrocławia. Jak tylko zdarza się okazja, przesyłam coś przez przyjeżdżających tutaj.

[...] Strajk zaczyna się coraz bardziej organizować, krzepnąć. Już w tej chwili my w drukarni myślimy o papierze na jakieś dwa tygodnie naprzód [*śmieje się*], żeby go nie zabrakło. Andrzej [Butkiewicz] dzwoni do mnie dzisiaj i mówi: *„Słuchaj, załatwiaj papier, bo już tylko na tydzień wystarczy"*.

[7]

Oświadczenie dziennikarzy:

My, polscy dziennikarze, obecni na Wybrzeżu Gdańskim w czasie strajku, oświadczamy, że wiele informacji dotychczas publikowanych, a przede wszystkim sposób ich komentowania, nie odpowiada istocie zachodzących tu wydarzeń. Taki stan sprzyja dezinformacji. Istniejąca blokada telekomunikacyjna oraz brak możliwości publikowania materiałów przedstawiających prawdziwy obraz sytuacji, dotyka nas boleśnie i uniemożliwia uczciwe wypełnianie obowiązków zawodowych.

Fot. Zbigniew Trybek

Dziennikarze przygotowują swoje oświadczenie

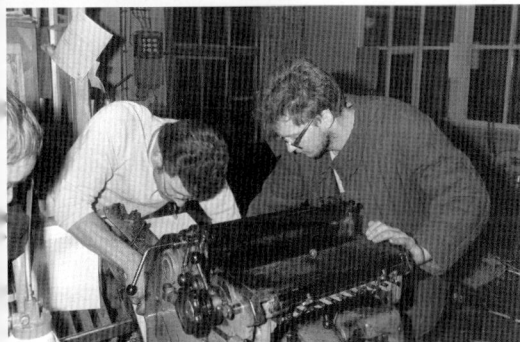

Niezależne drukarnie w stoczniach w Gdańsku i w Gdyni

Piotr Halbersztat (reporter z Polskiej Kroniki Filmowej):

Lekkie brawa. Specjalnie patrzyłem na reakcję sali. O entuzjazmie trudno by było mówić. Nawet jakiejś spontanicznej reakcji też nie było. Obok mnie siedziała grupa ze Stoczni Remontowej. Jeden z robotników popatrzył na mnie i powiedział: *„No, nareszcie, powrót synów marnotrawnych"*. Na zasadzie: rychło w czas się obudzili, ale dobre i to. Taka właśnie była rola, którą spełniło oświadczenie. Uratowanie resztki godności. [17]

Krzysztof Jagielski (Polskie Linie Oceaniczne, Szczecin):

Sala nie mogła pomieścić wszystkich. Przybyło nadspodziewanie wielu marynarzy. Stali na schodach i korytarzu. [...] Panowie z dyrekcji wymieniali między sobą uwagi, przeglądali jakieś papiery i nie zwracali uwagi na Hunderta, tak jakby nie istniał. W tej zatłoczonej sali zdawał się być sam. Wynik spotkania był niepewny. Odgadywałem, o czym myślał. Podjął przecież ryzyko strajku. [...] Czy go poprą? Jeżeli nie, wiado-

was no doubt how it would finish – he would be sacked, and left with an employment exclusion record.

[...] Hundert, as the representative of the work-force hosting this meeting, should be its chairman. *"What is he waiting for?"* I asked myself. [...] At last it was Director Rosicki who spoke. [...]

The blood rushed to my head, my heart was in my throat. I totally lost control. I heard my own deafening roar: *"Who is chairing this meeting? Are we striking or not striking? You have no right to speak! We make our own decisions here!"*.

[...] That roar of mine had the effect of a grenade thrown into an ammunition store. [...] *"Strike! Strike! Strike!"*; *"Let's choose a committee!"*; *"Jagielski to the Presidium!"*.

[22]

Photo: Jerzy Undro/ADM/PAP

Teresa Łyszkowska (teacher from Gdynia, temporarily in Warsaw):

I tried to telephone my husband in Gdynia to find out how things really are over there. Unfortunately, after many hours of unsuccessful attempts to get through, I gave up. I went to the post office, where I found out that it is impossible to get a connection. So I asked to send a telegram. I was told that neither telegrams nor registered letters are accepted for Gdynia. You can only send an ordinary letter.

[20]

Bogusław Krawczyk (fitter, Repair Yard in Szczecin):

Some of the demands were settled, but the most important ones – not. Talks were interrupted because the Deputy Prime Minister did not have the power to make decisions in some areas of conflict. [...]

The food provision situation in the Shipyard is very good, we have everything we need. But the atmosphere is more tense, as though something were about to erupt. We are a little tired, not physically, but psychologically. But nobody lets on. There are fears as to what will happen next. People are afraid of intervention by foreign powers.

Romuald Laskowski (Marine Repair Yard in Świnoujście):

Today a Soviet Dakota from a nearby airfield in the German Democratic Republic hovered over the Shipyard at a height of some 200 metres, observing us carefully. It circled round the perimeter many times, veering more and more to allow the observers sitting inside a better view. But nobody was worried – the workers carried on fishing. [20]

Extract from a declaration and appeal by the KSS "KOR":

The main cause of these arrests [12 members and associates of KOR] was the persistent work of KSS "KOR" to break the blockade of information about the strikes, their progress, the demands of the workers. [...] We demand the immediate release of those arrested.

We appeal to the entire public to support this demand. Foremost, we ask the Strike Committees to demand the release of all the dissident activists who have been arrested. They acted for the benefit and in the interest of the striking work-forces.

Photo: Grzegorz Nawrocki
Freedom for political prisoners

Z posiedzenia Sekretariatu KC PZPR:

1. Plan działań organizatorskich po IV Plenum KC PZPR.

[...]

Prezydium Rządu podejmie w najbliższym czasie następujące problemy:

– dla poprawy zaopatrzenia w mięso podejmie się z rezerw 40 tys. ton mięsa, co polepszy zaopatrzenie rynku we wrześniu o 3 punkty;

– podjęto decyzję o zakupie na rynkach zagranicznych środków do utrwalania jakości wędlin;

– przystąpi się do poszukania możliwości zaimportowania 30 tys. ton mięsa;

– proponuje się przywrócić system bonów na cukier;

[...]

– na Wybrzeżu, w stoczniach, prowadzić rozmowy zmierzające do wyraźnego opowiedzenia się, po której stronie są strajkujący. Należy zaproponować i przeprowadzić tajne głosowanie w stoczniach w sprawie podjęcia prac bądź dalszego strajku. W przypadku odrzucenia propozycji tajnego głosowania należy fakt ten wygrać propagandowo jako używanie metod niedemokratycznych i wywieranie nacisku na tych, którzy chcą podjąć pracę. Jeśli wniosek o podjęciu pracy uzyska większość, a mimo to strajk będzie się przedłużał, to też należy to pokazywać publicznie. Gdyby zaś za strajkiem opowiedziała się większość, to uzyskamy również informację, jaki procent załóg był za rozpoczęciem pracy, co stanowić będzie podstawę do określenia sił popierających partię i prowadzenia pracy wyjaśniającej, a także pokazywania złej woli kierujących strajkami.

– należy doprowadzić do sytuacji, w której komitety strajkowe niech dyskutują, natomiast załogi podejmą pracę, ruszą stocznie i porty;

[...]

– przygotowanie w środkach masowego przekazu wystąpień ludzi z autorytetem (tow. Wojna, tow. Rakowski);

– podjęcie przygotowań do spotkania tow. Edwarda Gierka z kardynałem Wyszyńskim.

[1]

Z teleksu sekretariatu KW w Gdańsku do Stanisława Kani:

Uwagi dotyczące formuły [rozmów z MKS-em]:

1. Zmiana w stosunku do pierwszej tury rozmów formy zachowań (werbalnych i gestu). Potrzebna „dyplomatyczna agresywność" w celu przejęcia inicjatywy lub osiągnięcia równowagi, elementy lżejsze np. „zastanówmy się";

[...]

3. Obniżenie rangi przewodniczącego poprzez zwracanie się do członków komisji [MKS] wg wariantów:

a. z nazwiskiem,

b. bez nazwiska;

[...] 5. Konieczność opracowania takiej formuły odpowiedzi na szczegółowe propozycje, aby przełamać barierę psychiczną i uzyskać aplauz sali i stoczni;

[...] 8. Konieczność przemyślenia formy wejścia na salę obrad – dojazd do sali nie autokarem a samochodem (wielkość samochodu dostosowana do wielkości ekipy). Wjeżdżać pierwszą bramą. [1]

Fot. Wojciech M. Druszcz

Z protokołu posiedzenia egzekutywy KM PZPR w Gdyni:

E. Lech [?], I sekretarz KZ PZPR RADMOR-u zwrócił uwagę na brak szybkiej i rzetelnej informacji, który powoduje, że nasza praca nic nie daje. Przeciwnik posiada ją i odnosi sukcesy. [...] Pracujemy w konspiracji i w każdym punkcie przegrywamy. Za kilka dni zajdzie potrzeba ukrywania się, a oni będą nas wyciągali.   [3]

Z meldunku komendanta miejskiego MO w Gdańsku płk. H. Stasiaka:

Uzyskano informację, że niejaka [...], będąc na uroczystości urodzinowej u swojej siostry [...], w obecności gości wypowiadała się bardzo krytycznie i w sposób wulgarny: *„Jak ma być w Polsce dobrze, jeżeli do PZPR idą sami debile, do milicji sami głupole i półgłówki, a w rządzie siedzą sami wariaci i osły"*. Oświadczyła, że takie jest jej przekonanie i będzie o tym głośno mówić.

[...] Ponadto dowiedziałem się, że stoczniowcy, którzy chcieliby podjąć pracę, terroryzowani są przez członków MKS, dokonuje się ich „aresztowań" i umieszcza w bunkrze pod budynkiem dyrekcji. Jest to informacja niepotwierdzona.

[...] Z uwagi na dochodzące uwagi krytyczne odnośnie wyglądu funkcjonariuszy w mundurach polowych typu „moro", zwrócić uwagę przy odprawach do służby na wygląd tychże milicjantów.   [4]

Fot. Jan Kups

Strajkujący stoczniowcy.
Druga od prawej Ewa Osowska

26-08-1980
wtorek

- *Druga tura rozmów gdańskiego MKS z Komisją Rządową.*
- *W Szczecinie ukazuje się pierwszy numer strajkowego pisma „Jedność" (z datą 24 sierpnia).*
- *Strajk solidarnościowy komunikacji miejskiej i zakładów pracy w Łodzi i we Wrocławiu.*

Andrzej Jakubowicz (DOLMEL, Wrocław):

Gorączkowo przekazywano sobie każdą, choćby najdrobniejszą informację nadchodzącą z Wybrzeża, wszyscy byli napięci do granic – pamiętano Grudzień. Całe miasto szykowało się do strajku powszechnego. Tak że w dniu, w którym miała stanąć komunikacja miejska, ludzie jadąc rano do pracy bez większych zakłóceń byli jakby zawiedzeni. Lecz około godziny 10.00 wszyscy już wiedzieli – zaczęło się.

[...] Tłumy gromadziły się przed zajezdniami, by na własne oczy ujrzeć biało-czerwone flagi, opaski na rękach straży robotniczej, by zamienić choć kilka słów z pracownikami okupującymi swoje miejsca pracy. Z godziny na godzinę przyłączały się kolejne zakłady, przeważnie ogłaszając strajki okupacyjne, nawet taksówkarze, ba, nawet skup makulatury, na którego bramie porozwieszano święte obrazki, czynem głosili swoją solidarność.

Marianna Waliszewska (Gdańsk):

26 sierpnia centrala telefoniczna zadzwo-niła do mnie i jakaś miła pani powiedziała: *„Przywrócono pani łączność".* Spotkała mnie miła niespodzianka. Międzymiastowa pomyłkowo połączyła jakiegoś pana z Wrocławia z moim mieszkaniem. Najpierw powiedziałam temu panu, że to pomyłka, a potem przeprowadziłam taką rozmowę:

– Czy Wrocław strajkuje?

– Połowa, proszę pani.

Pytanie tego pana:

– Czy was w Gdańsku mordują?

– Nie, a was?

– Niech by tylko spróbowali! [...]

Rozpłakałam się ze szczęścia, że nie jesteśmy chociaż teraz sami. [20]

Małgorzata Chmielecka (Sopot):

Tłumy ludzi, chociaż pogoda wcale nie sierpniowa. Za chwilę zaczną się rozmowy Komisji Rządowej z MKS-em. Każdy przemyka się bliżej bramy, żeby lepiej słyszeć. Obywa się bez uwag: „Panie, gdzie się pan tak pcha". Atmosfera wzajemnej życzliwości. Jeden drugiemu użycza parasola. Po prostu solidarność. [20]

Fot. Bogusław Nieznalski

Extract from talks between the Inter-factory Strike Committee and the Government Commission:

Lech Wałęsa:

We want free, independent and truly self-governing unions. There is a difficult and critical economic situation in the country. This came about because the world of work did not have its own, real union representation. [...]

Mieczysław Jagielski:

[...] This matter was dealt with at the recent plenum of the Central Committee of our Party. [...] It was said that the matter of reform of the activities of trade unions is an important and urgent task. [...] It is essential to take steps, which would radically improve the situation and which would enable the trade movement to strengthen its working class nature and to renew its position among the masses. [...]

Andrzej Gwiazda:

For many years the whole of the Polish economy, the local hierarchy and the branch authorities have been accountable according to how much steel they produce, how much coal, how many metres of cable. Nobody held them accountable for how the worker manages, how the teacher manages, how the engineer manages, or the office worker. Trade unions did exist, their primary aim the defence of the working people. But these unions never did defend their interests, in fact quite the opposite – dominated as they were by the enterprises' management, they went hand in glove with the directors and listened with trepidation to whispered words from the shop floors, whispered words of complaint. [...] Our aim is to form an organisation, which would truly be a workers' organisation, which people would find credible.

Lech Sobieszek:

[...] I believe – I really don't want to poke fun at anybody – but I really do believe that there must have been some sort of misunderstanding. Quite simply, we are asking for free trade unions and the Prime Minister [insists] on his condition of modernising the old ones. That's not what it's all about, really. That's just – as we say in Polish – "turning the matter inside out". I'm sorry to have to say this. [...]

Mieczysław Jagielski:

I would have you know that I am not insisting on the old unions, at all. In fact, I did say that I believe that this must, indeed, happen – I, too, was expressing my opinion on the subject – that there must be a reform of the activities of the trade unions.

Andrzej Gwiazda:

[...] and we are very happy to welcome these changes and the proposed reform of the present trade unions. After all, once we set up ours, our very own, then we will have to co-operate closely with these trade unions. [...] We are convinced that then these existing unions will also have to change.

Photo: Zbigniew Trybek

Photo: Zbigniew Trybek

Lech Wałęsa (after the government commission has left, having proposed that the first demand should be discussed in working groups):

They'll make their decisions, they'll come back, show us and we will read them through. If they're good, then OK, if not – well, then, we'll just carry on (*clapping*). And that is why I suggest, as we have not sung the National anthem yet today – let us once more give voice to our strong unity (they sing the anthem). And that is why I also propose we take a rest. This is likely to take time, because we do, in reality, want nothing other than entirely free unions, so they'll have a lot to agree on, quite a battle. But we will not resign from this point. [9]

Ministry of the Interior Staff Command proposals for operation "Summer 80":

From our investigations it would appear that the so-called Inter-factory Strike Committee in Gdańsk is becoming increasingly active and aggressive, it has been infiltrated by counter-revolutionary elements and the activities of this group are bent on forcing through a general strike in Poland. [...]

Under the circumstances, Ministry of the Interior Staff Command proposes that the following law-and-order and repressive actions be undertaken:

1. The Polish Navy to put the Northern Port in Gdańsk and the Port in Świnoujście back in action, which should have a psychological and economic effect.

2. The Shipyard in Gdańsk to be blockaded by units of the ZOMO (Mechanised Riot Militia) with a concurrent ultimatum that they [!] be vacated by the remaining work-forces still in occupation. [...]

4. The isolation of the active anti-socialist element, by way of warrants of arrest issued by the relevant prosecutors' offices and the subsequent issue of charges. [...]

The Staff Command of the Ministry of the Interior has made provision to place all forces and means at the disposal of the Ministry of the Interior on full alert. The mobilisation of reserve forces subject to the Department of the Interior is also envisaged (some 3,000). [2]

Extract from minutes of a meeting of the Politburo of the Central Committee of the Polish United Workers Party:

Comrade Stanisław Kania:

The situation is indeed very dangerous. But we cannot contemplate any means other than political methods. There has been no disturbance of public order. There are about 4,000 people inside the Gdańsk Shipyard and some 2,000 outside the gates. If we even attempted to detain the Inter-factory Strike Committee, then the crowd would be up in arms with the cry "hands off the Shipyard". [...]

Comrade Mieczysław Jagielski:

The strike in Gdańsk is a general strike, entirely supported by the public. If anything is still working, then it does so with the agreement of the Inter-factory Strike Committee. [...] They show no signs of weariness – their popular slogan is "we're still happy to be on strike". In front of the gates there is an angry, dangerous crowd, inside the Shipyard some 6,000 people are camping under make-shift tents. Today's meeting was concluded after some difficult negotiations. I was asked what news I have to bring them. [...] I read out to them clearly our point of view. It was rejected.

[...] The crux of the matter throughout the talks boils down to their basic question – will we agree to free, self-governing trade unions? Today they still pose the question, tomorrow they may no longer ask us. Time is not on our side. [...]

Slogan on banner: Man's good – the foremost aim of the Party

I am deeply convinced that if we do not agree to the formation of the new unions, Gdańsk will continue to strike.

[...]   [1]

Comrade Kania:

[...] Let us consider other valid political realities, as for instance: Cardinal Wyszyński's statement – consider, what will be the likely results of it; Wojna's comments about the scope of our compromises. These are all new concepts, which may influence any offensive from the Party and the active members.

[...] We should hold back before making a final decision. Up our sleeves, we still have the appeal planned in conjunction with the ZSL (United People's Party) and the SD (Democratic Front) under the banner of "our Socialist Nation in danger", which can be supplemented with spectacular events.

I would propose that we do not, as yet, give the impression of having conceded the matter of the formation of a new structure. But, between ourselves, we should not make even this stance too definite – it is better to take a step to the right than a step into the abyss. [...]

Comrade Andrzej Żabiński:

We should take immediate steps to draw the Party into a political battle. We must call a consultation of active Party members.

Comrade Edward Gierek:

A consultation in Warsaw – no; but we can do it in the Provinces.

I was expecting more positive news from Gdańsk. They aim to set up two parallel unions – class based and self-governing. Today they demand unions, they will grow in strength and then they will launch an attack on the Party, the government, the Sejm (Lower House). [...]

But Comrades, do we have the right to hand over power – even in the face of a general strike?   [24]

From a television appearance by Ryszard Wojna:

At the IV Plenum of the Central Committee we came to the conclusion that the situation in our country is developing in a dangerous direction. Unfortunately, this direction remains unchanged. Despite all efforts to the contrary, we still cannot say that we have managed to stem the tide of events, which may lead our country to a national disaster.   [8]

Extract from telexes from the Provincial Committees to the Central Committee of the Polish United Workers Party:

Olsztyn:

It was stated [at a consultative meeting of the Provincial Committee of the Polish United Workers Party] that our most committed Comrades, who hold responsible positions in everyday life, should not bow to a general mood of apathy and depression; they should continue their dialogue with working people and not hide their heads in the sand.

[...] The participants in the consultative meeting agreed that one of the conditions to holding a dialogue with society is the necessity of improving supplies of heating fuels, ensuring the availability of basic foodstuffs, a tight control on prices of food items for factory canteens and improvement in their supply.

Photo: Romuald Broniarek

Poster reads: PZPR – Polish United Workers Party

Płock:

During the night, a consignment of leaflets came in by train to Płock from the Gdynia Free Printing Press (21 demands of the Inter-factory Strike Committee). Already there is uncertainty in the new factories.

During the night between 25th and 26th August, some windows were smashed in the Power Station. Płock's only member of the Central Committee works there. It is not known whether this had anything to do with the incident.

Legnica:

In the Legnica province, during the night of 25th and 26th August, there was a positive socio-political atmosphere.   [1]

75

Photo: ADM/PAP

Cardinal Stefan Wyszyński at the Monastery in Jasna Góra

Photo: Erazm Ciołek

Extract from Cardinal Stefan Wyszyński's homily from the Jasna Góra Monastery in Częstochowa (the underlined text was removed by the Censor's office from the televised version):

We know well that, where honest work is absent, then even the most efficient economic system will fail and loans and debts will multiply. [...]

Although man has a right to rest, although in some cases, where there is no other way – he has the right to signal his views, even by desisting from work, we realise that this is a very costly argument. [...] Work in a trade or profession is not only a factor of economics, it is also a social and moral factor, closely tied with the spiritual development of man. If that development is cultivated then the whole economy of a nation becomes healthier.

That is why work, and not inactivity is man's ally [...]

However, in order that we may fulfil our duties, the sovereignty of the nation, of society, culture and of the economy are essential! [...] And although, today, complete sovereignty of nations forming various alliances and blocks is lacking, nevertheless, such alliances must have boundaries, the boundary of responsibility for one's own nation, for its laws and thereby its right to sovereignty.

From a meeting of the General Council of the Polish Synod of Bishops, held at Jasna Góra, under the chairmanship of Cardinal Wyszyński:

The General Council of the Polish Synod of Bishops pays tribute to both the striking workers and their committees, as well as to the authorities, for not allowing the situation to escalate to public disorder. This is proof of their civic and political maturity.

[...] While calling for order, peace and deliberation, [the Council] makes particular note and reminds everyone that a condition of internal peace is respect for the unalienable rights of the Nation.

27-08-1980

Wednesday

- *Negotiations in Gdańsk continue in working groups; the Inter-factory Strike Committee now includes over 500 striking factories and enterprises.*
- *During talks in Szczecin, Kazimierz Barcikowski throws out the demand to set up free trade unions.*
- *Sympathy strikes by factories and enterprises in Wałbrzych.*

Photo: Zbigniew Trybek

From a meeting of the Inter--factory Strike Committee:

Attention, we have an announcement: on 27th August, during the night, an attempt was made to enter the grounds of the Gdynia III Electro-Thermal Power Station on Pucka Street in the Gdynia-Chylonia district. A group of militiamen dressed in workers' boiler suits – most probably for the purposes of carrying out an act of sabotage. The group was stopped and, once their papers had been checked, they were expelled from the grounds. In view of the above, we ask you to be extra vigilant in all factories and workplaces where there is a sit-in strike.

Włodzimierz Mękarski ("Mostostal", Wrocław):

A fork lift truck arrived. I stood on a pallet. The truck lifted me up. Before me is a sea of heads. I begin to read out the proclamation issued by the Inter-factory Strike Committee. Suddenly everything began to happen of its own volition. A strike was proclaimed. [...] People began to set up flags around the factory, they made red and white armbands, closed the gates, organised food provisions, communications, a small printing press. I really don't know where this excellent organisation came from. After all, we had had no experience. Nobody had shown us how.

Extract from an article entitled "With whom do we speak" (from the "Solidarność Strike Information Bulletin"):

Gentlemen! You are speaking to different people - not to those who, in December 1970, answered the question "Will you help?", with "We will help!".
We are different above all because, being united, we have ceased to be powerless.
We are different because for the last 30 years we have been taught that promises are not kept.

Photo: A4 Photo/Pressfoto

78

Jerzy Janiszewski (artist, designer of the "Solidarność" logo):

I applied to the Inter-factory Strike Committee. [...] I looked round the conference room. Visual chaos: everywhere you looked, stacks of papers. A dearth of signs and slogans on the tables, behind which delegates to the Strike Committee from the various workforces sat and slept. I began to think how to bring order to this chaos. I thought of Inter-factory Strike Committee badges which would help to identify people. [...] I wanted to create a symbol, a meaningful sign.

I do not remember when it was that the idea of a graphic symbol actually came to me. Probably one night between the second and third round of talks. The concept arose from the following train of thought: just as the people in a unified crowd lean on each other [...], so the letters of the word should lean on each other, hold each other up. I began to hurry. I wanted to complete the fine details of this concept before the arrival of the Government Committee, so that they would realise it, too.
[29]

Photo: Stanisław Markowski

Extract from a memorandum sent by Father Hilary Jastak to Cardinal Stefan Wyszyński:

[...] All the faithful and I are surprised at the passive stance of the Polish Synod of Bishops in relation to matters of importance to the Polish nation. The public of the Coastal Provinces and all of us awaited a directive from the Episcopy as to special prayers, supplications for internal peace and a just solution to the demands made of the Polish People's Republic by the working people.

The passivity of the Episcopy of Poland, during this special time, in relation to the working people is all the more painful since one of the demands made by the strikers, and contained in point 3, is the provision of access to the mass media for representatives of all faiths.

It is bitter irony that, within this context, the freedom of speech in the mass media achieved for the Church at a cost of the lives of working people, and of which Your Eminence took advantage on 26th August 1980, should have been turned against those very working people.

The public of the Coastal Provinces has voiced an immediate and spontaneous reaction to its disappointment, putting us – the priests of the Coastal Provinces – in a very difficult situation.

[...] The reaction of the Party leaders in the Coastal Provinces was significant, as they busied themselves with their campaign against the working people, making reference to the arguments contained in the Cardinal's speech, printed by the Party press in the Coastal Provinces.
[8]

Extract from the minutes of a meeting of the Gdańsk Provincial Committee of the Polish United Workers Party, chaired by Deputy Prime Minister Jagielski:

Comrade Professor Antoni Rajkiewicz (advisor to Comrade Gierek):

[...] The password is free trade unions but, after some discussion yesterday, they agreed to the formula "self-governing unions".

From discussions carried out in the meantime, I know that acceptance of the negotiated proposition gives a 90 percent guarantee of a return to work.

[...]

Comrade Mieczysław Jagielski:

Comrades Fiszbach, Zieliński and I went to Warsaw yesterday. We reported on the situation – we do not have agreement for the formation of self-governing trade unions. I propose we conclude our discussion. [3]

Antoni Rajkiewicz:

In the morning, on his return from Warsaw, Jagielski calls a closed meeting of the members of the Government Commission and its experts and advisors. He is not in a good mood. He begins by saying that calls to end the conflict in Gdańsk by force are being voiced and to this end he asks all those present to make their personal views on the subject known. It turns out that none of those present opts for this solution with regard to the Shipyard; there is not, however, a consensus of opinion as regards the Northern Port.

[...] During a break in discussions by the negotiating group, Lech Wałęsa asked me for a word and told me: *"You are going to Warsaw, well then tell them top guys that we know that paratroopers have arrived and that they're preparing to storm the Shipyard. We don't want a violent confrontation and blood to be spilt. We'll defend ourselves".* [31]

Extract from minutes of meeting of the Politburo of the Central Committee of the Polish United Workers Party:

Comrade Stanisław Kania:

Our stance should be firm, although it may, perhaps, have serious repercussions. That is why we must issue an immediate declaration today by the Party and our allies. We must also resort to other means, like legal sanctions against people engaging in anti-socialist activities; Poland is at stake here. The organisers (Michnik, Kuroń, Moczulski) are detained for 48 hours at a time. We are also looking into the possibilities of taking the Northern Port and the Port in Świnoujście by force. This task cannot be given to the army. We are investigating the possibility of the Civil Militia carrying this out. This is not an easy or simple matter. We must also take note of the possible consequences. And even if we do take these ports – what then? Who will run them? We need professionals. We must take active steps to prevent people, firmly but tactfully, from massing in front of the Shipyard gates. Forcing an entry into the Shipyard is not a realistic answer, it would not achieve much and could lead to blood being spilt.

It appears that we must apply stronger censorship control ("Sztandar Młodych", in an article entitled "What do the workers want?" today published all their demands – the inclusion of this article was sanctioned by an employee of the Press Department of the Central Committee).

Comrade Jerzy Waszczuk:

Part of the print circulation of the "Sztandar Młodych" was stopped in Warsaw. The mechanics of censorship have been sharpened but will be further reinforced. But it should also be noted that a mood of criticism is growing in journalistic circles. [1]

Photo: Henryk Rosiak/ADM/PAP

From telephone conferences with the First Secretaries of the Provincial Committees of the Polish United Workers Party:

Comrade Edward Gierek:

[...] I am getting the message that, in the last several days, or so, Party activity within the Provincial Committees has greatly increased; where, at the beginning of the crisis, this was somewhat difficult and we found it difficult to mobilise ourselves, we are now finding new resources almost everywhere [...].

We are going to have to carry this burden on our shoulders for some time to come. [...]

Comrades, I know that this is difficult for you. I know that you have sleepless nights. I know that you are working hard – you, the executive committees, the Party apparatus and the Party activists, as well as Party organisations within factories and other enterprises, but try not to give way to despair, that will not help you in your work; try to believe that what you are doing is right. [1]

Extract from telexed information from the Gdańsk Provincial Committee to the Central Committee of the Polish United Workers Party:

Cardinal Stefan Wyszyński's homily has been accepted with understanding and approval. Party activists state that the text of the speech complemented our own activities. Surprise has been expressed that some parts of the speech were identical to that of Comrade Gierek in his public appearance. Activists state that we will probably be forced to make compromises with regard to the Church. [...] The homily is said to have been inspired. [1]

From information from the Ministry of the Interior:

Following the Cardinal's appearance, Bishop Tokarczuk in the presence of several bishops said that he would "never again sit down at the same table with him" and, indeed, during an official dinner, he pointedly sat at another table. [2]

Extract from a note of a conversation between the East German Deputy Minister of Public Security, Markus Wolf, with Deputy Ministers Stachura and Milewski of the Ministry of the Interior of the Polish People's Republic, and the Director of Department I of the Ministry of the Interior, Słowikowski:

The key aim of the political and operational centre is to weaken the counter-revolution centre in Gdańsk. [...] The main political demands of the strikers – free and self-governing unions – are seen as a demand to set up a legal opposition within the state. This cannot and will not be fulfilled.

[...] Our comrades in the Ministry of the Interior believe that, after several days of a successful political campaign, negotiations with the central strike committee will be broken off.

[...] There are signs of weariness among the strikers, who are beginning to wake up. Our Comrades have agents through whom they work and from whom we have news of the tactics employed by the strike leaders and of the atmosphere among the strikers. They hope that their activities will help to undermine the unity of the strikers, to return to talks with the strike committees and to deepen the isolation of the counter-revolution centre in the Lenin Shipyard, in order to combat it effectively.

[...] Our Comrades from the Ministry of the Interior are working intensively on the above solution; they do however, realise that this may lead to an escalation of the situation and to demonstrations and a general strike. They reckon that the situation should be assessed on a 50:50 basis. [18]

Extract from information from the Provincial Headquarters of the Civil Militia to the Ministry of the Interior:

Chinese workers at "Chipolbrok" are still evidencing considerable interest in the strike situation, in public tempers and in the striking factories and enterprises. They regularly follow reports in Polish newspapers and listen to broadcasts by Polish radio and television. Every day, all the Chinese gather at 22.00 hours for meetings, the contents of which are unknown. Unidentified people make regular clandestine visits to the Consulate. [4]

28-08-1980

Thursday

- *Third round of talks between the Gdańsk Inter-factory Strike Committee and the Government Commission.*
- *Strikes spread throughout Kraków and Wrocław; strike breaks out in the "July Manifesto" Mine in Jastrzębie.*

From talks between the Inter-factory Strike Committee and the Government Commission:

Andrzej Gwiazda:

Mr Prime Minister and Gentlemen of the Commission! Apparently we do not have political prisoners in this country. But can we have complete confidence in our judicial system in this matter? We have received guarantees of immunity for strike action, guarantees that those taking part in the strike and those associated with it will not face repercussions. But can we be sure that false witnesses will not be found and that the whole of the Inter-factory Strike Committee will not turn out to be a bunch of criminals? This matter arouses our deep anxiety (*clapping*).

We live in a country, in which the unity of the nation is dictated by the truncheons of the militia.

Mieczysław Jagielski:

Sir, those are far-reaching accusations.

Andrzej Gwiazda:

Far-reaching and possibly demagogical. Nonetheless 48-hour detainments, for people who hold views other than the official ones, are a matter of course.

[...] Society is afraid. Afraid of repercussions. [...] Fear exists – fear of speaking out during production meetings, at union meetings, fear of coming out with a more daring proposal. We must be rid of this. [...]

Mieczysław Jagielski:

You have made a statement, which has hurt me deeply. How can you say: do we have guarantees that the strikers here and the presidium will not be judged to be... I hesitate to even use your word "criminals". Let me tell you, this has wounded me personally. After all, the people I speak to here are all honest, extremely honest people. So, how could anyone treat the people here in such a way?

Lech Wałęsa:

Mr Prime Minister – I, myself, have suffered dozens of attempts to frighten me; have heard that when I leave here, then... this and that... And I am not the only one.

Mieczysław Jagielski:

Sir, in that case, even I should be hounded... [9]

Maciej Pietrzyk (actor and singer):

After my performance in the Health & Safety conference room, a girl came up to me, a girl who worked there as a typist. She gave me a piece of paper and said: *"Sing that, please, you must sing it"*.

I sat down "beneath Lenin" and within ten minutes I had composed some music to the words. And that is how the "Song for a Daughter" came about. I sang it with a shaky voice, Maciej Prus held up the paper with the words for me. People cried. Those simple words expressed the crux of all that the strikers felt. The poem was passed round in the Shipyard as an anonymous work. It later transpired that Krzysztof Kasprzyk was its author.

Maciej Pietrzyk sings "Song for a Daughter"; left: Maciej Prus

Photo: Zbigniew Trybek

Jadwiga Piątkowska (Gdańsk Shipyard):

We type till two, sometimes three at night. We sleep where we can, here in the conference room, on chairs. I volunteered to help because I wanted to make my own small contribution as a single mother. My daughter is 12 years old, she is at home by herself. She came to see me at the gate twice. We said as much as we could through the gate. But she understood and when she went off she indicated that everything was all right, that she would manage.   [13]

From a report by a delegate of striking factories in Elbląg:

On 28th August representatives of the Provincial Committee of the Polish United Workers Party entered the grounds of the management of the PKS (State Road Transport) branch in Elbląg. One of them, called Jamrozy, began to shout at Mr Hoffman, saying that he is sowing an ideological revolution. He said: *"You can strike for the next six months",* And then to the question *"Why, will you shoot at us?",* he answered: *"if needs be, we'll shoot".* So, while a member of the Politburo of the Polish United Workers Party and the Deputy Prime Minister of the Polish People's Republic, Mr Jagielski, talk with the Inter-factory Strike Committee, their Party colleagues try to terrorise our striking workers.   [8]

Leopold Sobczyński ("July Manifesto" Mine in Jastrzębie):

People came back from their holidays on the Baltic coast and told us about what was going on in the Triple City, in Szczecin. [...] The last straw for us was the behaviour of the Director of the Mine, who treated us like cattle. [...] When the second shift came up from the shaft, there was a sudden stir in the stamping room. Someone in the crowd shouted that the whole of the Coast is on strike while we sit tight like mummies. A strike committee was set up in total spontaneity.

[...] Telephone links with the Coastal Provinces were cut. We sent out some independent couriers. One of them was able to evade the patrols of the Security Police and the Coastal Provinces learned of our strike.

Performance by actors from the Teatr Wybrzeże (Seaside Theatre) in the Safety & Hygiene conference room

Photo: Zbigniew Trybek

Government Commission. Seated in the first row: Jerzy Kołodziejski, Tadeusz Fiszbach, Mieczysław Jagielski

Photo: Zbigniew Trybek

Extract from minutes of the visit of delegates from the Paris Commune Shipyard Strike Committee in Gdynia to Cardinal Stefan Wyszyński in Warsaw:

[...] The delegation was received at 11 a.m. in the conference room of the Polish Synod of Bishops, in the Primate's House, where it presented His Eminency with a letter from Father Hilary Jastak. [...] His Excellency thanked the "faithful children of the Fatherland" warmly for their loyalty, sacrifice and the trust they place in the Holy Mother of God, the Church and Her Priests. At the same time he stated that it was only now that he had seen the full, objective and honest picture of what was happening in Poland – on the Gdańsk coast.

Referring to the matter of his homily, which had caused so much misunderstanding, he explained that the text, which had been published, was not authorised, not complete, nor was its author asked for permission to publish it in the mass media of the Polish People's Republic.   [8]

Photo: ADM/PAP

Extract from minutes of a meeting of the Politburo of the Central Committee of the Polish United Workers Party:

Comrade Edward Gierek:

On behalf of the leadership of the USSR, Ambassador Aristov presented an official declaration, expressing concern at the developing situation in Poland. They consider that our counter-offensive is too ineffective, there is little evidence of Activist action and the tone of the press self-deprecatory or defensive. In the Coastal Provinces there are a great many foreign journalists who add fuel to the fire. They are surprised that we have not yet closed our borders to the West. He asked what solution do we foresee and how are we going to go about it. [...]

The tone of the declaration was quite categorical, it sounded like a warning, that danger is imminent. [...]

We must contact Comrade Jagielski and ask how the talks are going, and then control them in such a way as to lay the blame at their door at the appropriate moment.

In addition, it is essential:

– to tighten the blockade of the Coastal Provinces and introduce a state of emergency in the main centres, and, this very night, to carry out a series of arrests;

– to decide whether not to issue a directive tomorrow for all members of the Party to leave those premises which are striking.

In our propaganda we should stress that we have already considered and fulfilled the demands of the working people; and do not intend to consider the demands of people who are hostile to socialism.   [24]

From telexed information from Provincial Committees to the Central Committee of the Polish United Workers Party:

Gdańsk:

We have noted cases of losing active Party members, of confusion, lack of confidence in the permanency of the Party line and Party tactics: "perhaps something will change once again and we will once again lose face".

Płock:

Among older people, who have lived through the war, there is talk of concern at the consequences of the developing situation on the Coast. Questions were asked relating to the strikers: "Who are these people? They have no conscience, they want to destroy everything we have built".   [1]

From information from the Provincial Headquarters of the Civil Militia to the Ministry of the Interior:

It has been established that in the Gdynia Parish Office of Father Jastak, who has been frequently mentioned in reports, there is a large store of illegal printed material, including strike reports, appeals, bulletins etc., which he is distributing through the media of the church services and trusted Party activists. [4]

From a report by the City Commander of the Civil Militia in Gdańsk:

According to unconfirmed information, strike literature is being delivered to an ice-cream kiosk called "Miś" (Teddy Bear), situated near the suburban train station in Sopot. The staff of the kiosk deals with distribution of the literature. [4]

Extract from an article in "Pravda":

[...] The enemies of socialist Poland even go as far as, for instance, to print retaliatory statements in many West German newspapers, which contain – no more nor less than – a demand for the verification of Polish borders.

Feeding on the many subjective and objective problems which appear in the country, anti-socialist elements are attempting to pool their resources in order to push Poland off her chosen socialist path, which is so essential to the basic needs of the Polish nation.

Extract from a document written by Suslov's Commission – including: Suslov, Gromyko, Andropov, Ustinov and Chernienko

(underlined text indicates hand-written comments):

[...] Taking into account the situation which has developed, the Ministry of Defence [USSR] asks that, as a matter of urgency, three armoured divisions (1 in the Baltic Military District, 2 in the Byelorussian Military District) and one mechanised division (Transcarpathian Military District) be put on full battle alert by 18.00 hours on 29th August, in order to prepare troops, should armed intervention be required to help the Polish People's Republic.

[...] The successful entry of these divisions onto the territory of the Polish People's Republic requires that military preparation is undertaken approximately five to seven days in advance.

If the situation in Poland continues to deteriorate, we will also have to supplement the divisions of the Baltic, Byelorussian and Transcarpathian Military Districts, which are already on full alert to full battle readiness. Should the main forces of the Polish Army side with the counter-revolutionaries, we must supplement our own force by a further five to seven divisions. With this in mind, the Ministry should seek approval to call up an additional 75 thousand reserves, and to provide a further 9 thousand military vehicles.

In other words, this would mean the mobilisation of up to 100 thousand reserve troops and the requisition of 15 thousand vehicles from the national economy. [16]

Photo: Romuald Broniarek

WARSZAWA POZDRAWIA MOSKWĘ

Slogan on poster: Warsaw sends its regards to Moscow

29-08-1980

Friday

- *The impasse relating to the first point on the list of demands continues.*
- *The wave of sympathy strikes throughout the country grows (Upper and Lower Silesia, Kraków, Wrocław, Poznań, Bydgoszcz, Krosno, Łódź, Warsaw).*
- *At a secret meeting, the leadership of the Polish United Workers Party decides to continue talks with the strikers immediately, rejecting the alternative of an armed solution.*

Andrzej Gwiazda and Lech Wałęsa

Ireneusz Engler (television journalist):

Central propaganda was all the time presenting news as from another world, another country. My camera registered the following picture: the conference room with delegates from the striking work-forces, on the rostrum a television set, its cables torn out, dangling forlornly in front of the rostrum. The television nothing but a stage prop, which nobody watched or listened to. [17]

From discussions at a plenary meeting of the Inter-factory Strike Committee:

Bogdan Lis:

For the second time now the Government Commission has called off its plenary meeting with us. During today's telephone conversation, they said they were not ready and must first discuss certain matters, concerning the first point, in a working group. The working group is to arrive at 1.00 p.m. We, on the other hand, think we are simply being set up by the Government Commission.

Andrzej Gwiazda:

The Government Commission has deviated from the proposed practise of making all the discussions open – perhaps they need a pretext for breaking off talks. [9]

Iwona Skonieczna (Szczecin):

There are many people in the security post, whole families. The women unload jars, cigarettes and parcels from their bags. They watch the men's lips, as they eat. Quiet conversations, a lot of smoke.

The port workers are tired. Inactivity is killing them. Jurek cannot manage any warmth. I, too, am somehow tense. [21]

Krystyna Jagiełło (journalist):

A man came to the Inter-factory Strike Committee from a radio/television repair workshop and said that he and his colleagues had decided not to repair any more radios or televisions, seeing that radio and television lie so much. [17]

Andrzej Wajda:

The strikers' sentry post at the gate [to the Shipyard] recognised me and led me to the conference room, and one of the Shipyard workers told me straight out:

"You should make a film about us..."

"What film", I asked.

"Man of Iron", he answered without a moment's thought.

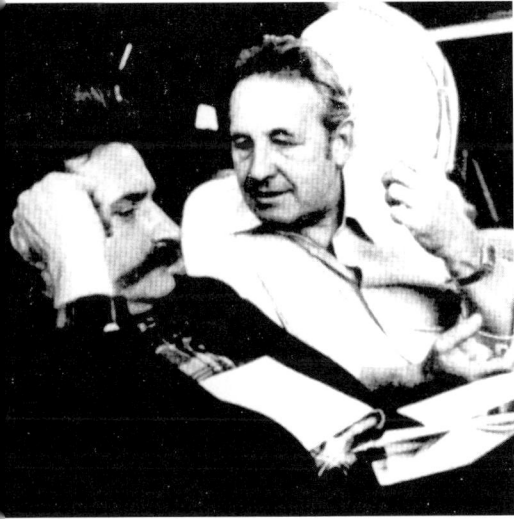

Lech Wałęsa and Andrzej Wajda

I had never made a film on demand, but I could not ignore this challenge. Memories of "Man of Marble" came to me, the final scene took place outside this very gate to the Shipyard. It could be a good beginning for a new film.

Aleksander Tuerner (economic technician, "Police" Chemical Works):

The sun is shining, it is warm. The sort of weather for a walk in the nearby forest, for instance. Nothing doing.

[...] At about midday, distressing news. The talks have been broken off! Apparently the Government Commission left and nobody knows when it will return. A general feeling of despondency. Weariness, particularly psychological, is only too evident. In some people this tenseness borders on the hysterical, in others it manifests itself in defeatism. [...]

[In the evening] the latest news is announced. Talks in the Warski Shipyard are to be undertaken this very night. [...] It is not till almost morning that we go to sleep on the blocks of expanded polystyrene. If only it were for the last time! [20]

Janusz Jachnicki (Test Workshop, Gdynia):

From a conversation overheard from the City Committee of the Polish United Workers Party in Gdynia, I learnt that, beyond the horizon stands the war fleet of our "brother nation", ready to intervene. My hair rose on end – I recalled what had happened in Hungary. In the morning I went to the Shipyard again. I met with

Borusewicz and Wałęsa, who became angry: *"Why don't they keep us informed?"* I understood then that the Inter-factory Strike Committee had some sort of unofficial contact with representatives of the authorities. Wałęsa's determination and immunity to stress made a big impression on me.

Piotr Halbersztat (Polish Television News journalist, staying in the Gdańsk Shipyard):

Friday 29th August was truly a day of dread for us. Suddenly, we all heard the news that arrests had commenced in Warsaw, Łódź and in Wrocław. It looked as if, despite negotiations being well under way, the authorities had nonetheless decided to use force. That's the way everybody understood it. In the Shipyard, someone came up to me and said: *"Listen, take your team and get out of the Shipyard. By evening at the latest"*. I asked what had happened, why leave? *"Tanks are likely to roll in during the night."* *"But, that's impossible, impossible"*, I said. I knew well that all was possible, still I did not want to believe it and said: *"I can't do that, we've been here from the start"*. [17]

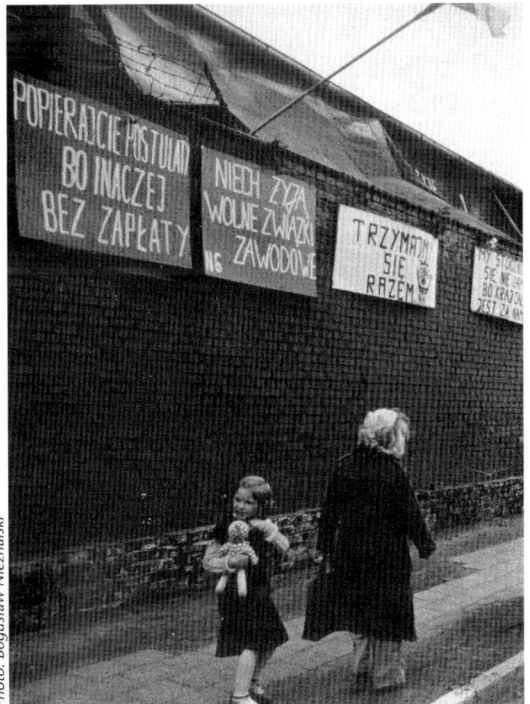

Photo: Bogusław Nieznalski

Slogans on the Shipyard walls: "Support the demands, without them no pay"; "Long live free trade unions"; "Let's keep together"

Extract from minutes of a meeting of the Politburo of the Central Committee of the Polish United Workers Party:

Comrade Edward Gierek:

The situation is increasingly grave, the strikes are spreading, demands escalating. I must confess I do not know what we can do, other than what we are already doing. The Party has been demobilised, it no longer believes that we can control the situation.

[...] As to those free trade unions – more and more people are declaring themselves in favour. I am against. But the situation is as it is, we are faced with the danger of a general strike. Perhaps we should choose the lesser of the evils, and then try to get out of it somehow. [...]

Comrade Tadeusz Kruczek:

We must consider declaring a state of emergency, and try to defend our power.

Comrade Józef Pińkowski:

I discussed the possibility of retaking the ports with Brych and Fiszbach today. The both said that it would end in battle. The Northern Port can be taken quite easily today, but how are we to run it tomorrow? The same with Szczecin and Świnoujście. If we take the ports by force, they might well turn on the Provincial Committees with force. [...]

Comrade Wojciech Jaruzelski:

There has been mention of declaration of a state of emergency – our Constitution does not make provision for this. We can only declare a state of Martial Law, but this we cannot do – how do we bring in restrictions when the whole nation faces up to us. This is not realistic. We must avoid issuing directives, which we cannot see through.

[...] What compromises can we accept? I do not know too much about union matters. As far as possible we should keep up talks, show our good will. The matter of the new structures should be discussed with our allies, because this is a matter of doctrine.   [24]

Extract from propaganda material of the Department of Ideology and Education of the Central Committee of the Polish United Workers Party:

In material sent to the Provincial Committee on 28th August [...] we indicated the presence of representatives of anti-socialist forces in the course of the strike events taking place in Gdańsk. We indicated that we would provide more detailed information on the main ringleaders.

With this material we are presenting details of several noteworthy individuals. The material should be used to bolster arguments in discussions with Party activists and workforces. It is, after all, essential to indicate with due credibility, who is behind the attempts to escalate tension. [...] In direct discussions it is necessary to stress the long-term involvement and deep-rooted loyalties of these people, noted for their anti-socialist

Photo: Mirosław Iringh/ADM/PAP

Slogan on poster: Our aim – a Socialist Poland

Photo: Romuald Broniarek

activities, with reactionary circles in the Federal German Republic, in England, France and the USA. It must be made clear that that is where the money comes from, which enables them to live well and not have to work. [1]

From a report by the City Commander of the Civil Militia in Gdańsk:

A shortage of the following has been noted: cooking oil, meat, vegetables and fruit, as well as: sugar, soap, detergent and hard goods.

At 12 noon, an announcement over the loudspeakers at the Gdańsk Shipyard said that the Government Commission had – once gain – refused to come to the Gdańsk Shipyard for further talks. [Wałęsa] said that he fears provocation on the part of the government side, in the form of a group of people sent in to the conference room in order to cause a disturbance. [4]

Extract from telexed information from the Provincial Committees to the Central Committee of the Polish United Workers Party:

Legnica:

I wish to inform you that the strike committee in the Provincial Public Transport Company in Legnica has taken a decision to expel members of the management board from the premises of the Company. The First Secretary of the Basal Party Organisation is still on the premises but when he appears among the strikers, they start to shout "Out with the Party".

Gorzów:

Yesterday evening, at the demand of the workforce, a meeting took place of a 200-strong group of workers of "SOWI" [?] with the First Secretary of the factory and the Director in Chief of the enterprise. [...] The participants obliged management to pass on the gist of the discussion, the questions raised, opinions and conclusions reached, to the provincial and central authorities.

We are now presenting them verbatim:

"It hurts to know that essential building work has been halted, the construction of the hospital cancelled, yet the Provincial Committee Building is going up, at a cost of many millions of zloties. Can the Party not make do with a more simple seat?" [...]

"The government is leading us straight into ruin. The government must make a stand, it must start to do something."

"On the television, they all say that we are in danger. Gierek talks about it, so does the Prime Minister and others. What is it? What are we in danger from?"

"Will we have to bear the consequences? That's the way it's been in the past."

"We are constantly lying to each other in this country."

"Sir, as the director, you tell us what we must do! After all, it would appear that our work to date has destroyed Poland. What next?"

Poznań:

The current crisis situation in Poznań bodes a general strike. According to an appraisal by the Office of the Secretary of the Provincial Committee of the Polish United Workers Party in Poznań, which was preceded by attendance on the district and town-and-country management of Party activities, as well as attendance on the largest factories and enterprises – it would unequivocally seem that the authority of the Party and the people's rule is decreasing. Against this background, in conversations and discussions throughout the whole of Poznań society – the authority of the First Secretary of the Central Committee of the Polish United Workers Party has been completely lost. [1]

The crowd before the gate was like a defensive shield. [...] That gate did not divide people, it united them.

Wojciech Adamiecki

A visit to the Shipyard was almost akin to a civic duty. I overheard the following conversation between a man and his wife in the vicinity of the railway station. She said: *"We're going to the Shipyard"*. He answered: *"I'm not going there. What's the point of pushing through that crowd with a child?"*. *"But we're in Gdańsk"*, she answered, *"we have to go to the Shipyard"*.

"And what good will standing in the crowd do?" he asked. *"Have you taken leave of your senses, it's your duty to go to the Shipyard and stand there for a while..."*

Ewa Juńczyk

[17]

30-08-1980

Saturday

- *Signing of an agreement in Szczecin and initialling the two first points in Gdańsk.*
- *V Plenum of the Central Committee of the Polish United Workers Party ratifies the Szczecin agreement and takes a decision to sign the agreement in Gdańsk.*
- *Strikes continue and spread throughout the country.*

Krzysztof Jagielski (Szczecin):

After six days the strike of the employees and sailors of Polish Ocean Lines in Szczecin was concluded. The office block emptied. Gusts of a warm breeze came through the open windows, lifting the scattered papers. I suddenly felt very tired. What next?

[...] I could not understand why we had not signed at the same time as Gdańsk. An unforgivable error. They are still on strike there. Poland is on strike. And if the strikes carry on for longer? We are bound by solidarity. Re-start the strike? And what if the Inter-factory Strike Committee does not agree? Disunity? Is that what the Communists were after? Most probably.

They succeeded in Szczecin. This is their victory – not ours. [...] A free union, like an island amidst a sea of hatred. What awaits us? [22]

Edmund Soszyński (Gdańsk Shipyard worker):

Saturday and the morning hours of Sunday were, to my mind, the most critical. People were extremely tired and were beginning to quarrel without reason at the hint of a discussion. News, or perhaps a rumour, reached us that Szczecin has signed and settled everything, while we are standing in the same place and it is not known how much longer we may be striking. [20]

Photo: Jerzy Undro/ADM/PAP

Signing the agreement in Szczecin. From left: Marian Jurczyk and Kazimierz Barcikowski

From discussions between the Inter-factory Strike Committee and the Government Commission:

Mieczysław Jagielski:

It may be that some people were losing patience on account of the long duration of the negotiations. One of the people, who ushered us in today and rode in our bus, said to me: "You're not here with us often enough, Mr Prime Minister". I believe that it is not about time but about the successful conclusion of our business and being able to move on.

[...] Our Party wants to be able to clearly emphasise today at a plenary meeting of the Central Committee its principled stand in the matters which we are discussing here... [...] Acceptance at that level will be the best guarantee of a political desire to see the accepted agreement through.

[...] Might it not be advisable to edit a suitable announcement, which would convey the thought that we have, in effect, worked out our differences and that we therefore intend that... whatever we feel is the most important point: and we are concluding the strike and getting back to work. We've actually already prepared a suitable announcement. Representatives could stay on here to amend it. I would come back this evening. [...] I would like to do so as early as possible, after all – people want to get some rest; it is, after all, Saturday today. [...]

Lech Wałęsa:

Mr Prime Minister, there really is not much more work on the most important points. The others we'll go through quickly. That is why I propose: we have waited so long, it's now Saturday, then Sunday, we'll work through it [...] and if all goes well, then we really do want to resume work on Monday, but we really must have every-thing clearly set down in writing.

Mieczysław Jagielski:

It will be in writing.

Lech Wałęsa:

Yes, it will be, but we want to have it (*laughter and clapping*).

[...] And I have another proposal. I would ask that somebody exert some influence and stop the arrests. In Warsaw, in particular, masses of people are being arrested – let's make no bones about it – they belong to KOR (clapping) but these people have done nothing wrong. They helped us, but they were not with us. They didn't do anything. So, we on our part will appeal to them not to spoil our work, because we are beginning to come to an agreement. But please, I beg you, don't arrest them, let them go free. If they do do wrong, then we ourselves may well be in favour of taking suitable action. [...] Honestly, we want you to come back, Mr Prime Minister. Except that, well, those applications for arrest... please do something about those Mr Prime Minister, so they don't happen.   [9]

Photo: Aleksander Jałosiński

Lech Wałęsa and Mieczysław Jagielski during talks in the Shipyard

Extract from minutes of a meeting of the Politburo of the Central Committee of the Polish United Workers Party:

Comrade Stanisław Kania:

Yesterday, Comrade Gierek had a discussion with Comrade Aristov on the matter of our stance concerning trade unions and he gave reasons for the necessity of achieving a compromise in this matter. We presented our opinion that these new structures are not good, but that the strike structure is even worse. We await the answer of our Soviet Comrades. Comrade Jagielski also took part in this meeting.

We have decided that an agreement will be signed after the Plenum. Despite the arrangement that signing would not take place before the Plenum makes its decision, Comrade Barcikowski went ahead and signed an agreement in Szczecin with the Inter-factory Strike Committee. In Gdańsk, Jagielski only initialled the agreement. This was a wilful act on the part of Comrade Barcikowski. Following the signing in Szczecin, there was a general feeling of euphoria, which we had expected.

Comrade Stefan Olszowski:

What happened in Szczecin was not good. As to the answer from our allies, we should wait, because they may delay their answer until Monday, Tuesday. [...]

Comrade Edward Gierek:

During our discussion yesterday, we actually presented it this way: that we inform them of our intentions but do not ask for advice. They might not express their doubts until two, three days hence. I believe we should call the Plenum meeting (without informing the Plenum of this conversation). [...]

Comrade Andrzej Werblan:

No speeches from the Plenum should be published, only an announcement that the meeting took place, heard the reports presented by the

Mieczysław Jagielski and Kazimierz Barcikowski

chairmen of both the Government Com-missions and accepted them. [...]

Comrade Władysław Kruczek:

Comrade Gierek's speech at the Plenum must contain an explanation as to why we have gone for this compromise.

Comrade Edward Gierek:

You are living in a world of illusions, you're not taking reality into account. And reality is that we have 700 thousand people on strike in the country today.   [1]

From a speech made by Mieczysław Jagielski at the V Plenum of the Central Committee of the Polish United Workers Party:

On the huge gate of the Gdańsk Shipyard hangs a sign "21 times YES". It concerns the 21 demands which, for many days, have been the subject of negotiations and – why deny it – mutual bartering. [...] The idea of free trade unions is, let us be quite clear, a dream for our enemies. [...] But for society – for the hundreds and thousands of shipyard workers and port workers, as well as representatives of other workers and working circles today it is – I put it forward and I firmly believe it – in their eyes, this is a real guarantee of the realisation of their demands and, at the same time, a guarantee that the degeneration or deformation of our socio-political and economic life will be over and done with.

From a speech made by Kazimierz Barcikowski at the V Plenum:

We [in Szczecin] made one mistake because when, sometime between two and three in the morning, we had come to an agreement with the presidium of the strike committee that we could sign the conclusion of the strike at eight, then we, Comrades, wanted to make it known in Warsaw that the strike was almost over and we telephoned our Comrades to let them know that this event was about to take place, and by that time all the shipyard workers knew that the agreement would be signed, and then we suddenly found out that we did not have the right to sign, we can only initial; but I'd give a prize to anyone in the Shipyard who can tell the difference between signing and initialling.

The matter of the strike is, above all, a matter of credibility. You really do have to battle for credibility in the words you use there.

[...] if we are to be responsible for the fact that the strike in Szczecin is over, then I am here, at your disposal.   [1]

Mieczysław Jagielski (in an interview in 1991):

I realised that agreement [to free trade unions] was an unprecedented about-turn, but refusal – a threat of national catastrophe. I was quite simply afraid – as a politician and as an individual – of what would happen, whether it would work and what will happen if it does not work.   [28]

From a speech by Janusz Brych, First Secretary of the Szczecin Provincial Committee of the Polish United Workers Party at the V Plenum:

I have before me an appeal to the nation, which was distributed among the members of the Central Committee during our meeting. Passing texts of appeals will not help us at this moment. They do not bring any results. I wish to declare that I will not be voting for its acceptance. I do, however, have one question for the leadership of our Party. What ideas do they have to get us out of this present predicament? Thank you.   [1]

Extract from an appeal by the Central Committee to members of the Polish United Workers Party:

Comrades!

We turn to you at this very special time. Our Fatherland is faced with a great danger.

[...] At this moment, when we are undertaking a great work of reform, hostile forces are intruding upon our dialogue, forces which aim to bring about a gradual change in the political system of Poland, to the detriment of the interests of the working classes.

[...]

Let us draw ranks.

Let us oppose the enemy of the working classes.

Let us work to bring back peace, order and the natural rhythm of life.

Comrades!

Conquer your hesitation and your indecisions!

Our actions today must be governed by superior rights.

Standing behind the Party we must turn about this dangerous run of events.   [1]

Photo: GAMMA/BEJW

Slogan: 21 x YES

Photo: Bogusław Nieznalski

From STASI information about the reactions and tempers of the Polish people:

[...] Many citizens are throwing aside Marxism-Leninism without knowing what it means. Revolutionary sensitivity is almost non-existent. This can be seen in the far-reaching effects of western influence in the field of ideology. Western tourists flock to Poland in droves and spread their ideologies here.

[...] As a result of ideological carelessness, the Party leadership was taken unawares by the events of recent months and did not react in time. Party organisations within the striking factories took hardly any action. Quite the contrary, numerous Party members joined the strikers.

[...] The "Polish mentality" does not allow for acceptance and carrying out of orders without discussion.

[...] Some citizens give the impression that part of society treated the events almost as a "game". They want to find out how far they can go, to win. Not everyone realises the gravity of the situation. [18]

31-08-1980

Sunday

From the final round of talks between the Inter-factory Strike Committee and the Government Commission:

Alina Pienkowska:

Please bear in mind the fact that these people, who are currently being arrested, in 1976 helped the families of workers sacked from the Shipyard. Workers still remember this, which is why they are appearing on behalf of the employees of the Gdańsk Shipyard and we ask for the immediate release of all those arrested or detained as a result of the strike.

Mieczysław Jagielski:

Once again I repeat my statement made in full consciousness of responsibility for the matter. I will go there and will pass this on. Even today I will report the matter in the way it was presented here. I am not empowered to do any more, other than what I do on my own responsibility and the dictates of my own conscience, I have no further power than that.

Andrzej Gwiazda:

Mr Prime Minister, we have faith in your good will. But the arrests still continue. We have at this moment information about new names. [...]

Mieczysław Jagielski:

We will add that list to our minutes. [...] I propose we carry on, so that we can get an idea of some of the other matters.

[After a break]

I am happy to announce that the Prosecuting authorities will make their decision regarding the release of people detained pending investigations and also those who figure on the list handed to me by the Inter-factory Strike Committee, after 12 noon tomorrow, i.e. 1st September 1980.

[...]

Lech Wałęsa:

Once again I would like to thank you, Mr Prime Minister, and all those involved, who did not allow the matter to be solved by the use of force and that we were able to come to an agreement as one Pole to another. Without the use of force. [...]

Dear Friends! Let us return to work on 1st September [...]. Have we achieved everything we wanted, everything we strived for, everything we dreamt of? I always speak honestly and say what I mean. And now I will be straight with you – not everything, but we are all aware that we have achieved a great deal. You trusted me throughout, now believe me when I say: we have achieved everything, which we could possibly achieve in the current situation. The rest we will also achieve because we have won the most important matter: our own independent, self-governing trade unions. They are our guarantee for the future.

[...] I declare the strike over.

Mieczysław Jagielski:

During the entire period of our mutual co-operation, we have tried to understand the motivation behind your actions. [...] We spoke as Poles should speak with one another. [...] There are no winners and no losers. There are no victors and no vanquished. [...] I repeat: we have reached agreement! [9]

Photo: Witold Górka

Photo: Archives of the Ministry of the Interior and Administrative Department

Extracts from minutes of a meeting of the Executive of the Provincial Committee of the Polish United Workers Party in Gdańsk held on 1st September 1980:

Comrade F. Pieczewski:

We must take stock and decide how we are going to re-build Party prestige. They had solidarity – that was their strength. [...] There are too many cliques in the Party. Today, after 30 years, I am considering handing back my Party membership card. [...]

Comrade T. Kuta:

We must, at all costs, avoid political battles. If anti-socialist overtones appear then we must not hesitate to prevent them spreading; however, we should not sniff them out where they do not exist. [3]

Extract from a telegram from Günther Sieber, Ambassador of the German Democratic Republic in Poland, commenting on the meeting held on 1st September 1980 between the Deputy Prime Minister, Mieczysław Jagielski, and Emil Wojtaszek, Minister for Foreign Affairs, with the Ambassadors of "fraternal" states:

[Comrade Jagielski]:

Comrade Ambassadors, the consequences of what has happened here, in our country, are obvious to us. We do, however, realise that your Parties may have their doubts. On behalf of our leadership, please explain that we had no other choice.

[...] During my speech in Gdańsk, I stated that there are no victors and no vanquished. Lenin once said that, in some cases, one must take a step back in order to be able to, then, move forward. We understand this. What has taken place here was that step backwards. [32]

Cryptogram from the Deputy Director of the Operations Office of Staff Headquarters of the Civil Militia, Colonel Józef Chudzik, to Provincial Commanders of the Civil Militia in Kraków, Łódź and Poznań (14.50 hours):

Very urgent

On the orders of the Staff Director of the Ministry of the Interior please send 20 men from the ZOMO (Motorised Riot Police) Special Platoon to Gdańsk. The men should be in civilian dress, without firearms, they should take their field uniforms with them, also climbing ropes, belts, fastenings, as well as standard engineering equipment. The men will be transported by helicopter. Details will follow by telephone. [4]

Photo: Zbigniew Trybek

Signing of Agreement between the Inter-Factory Strike Committee and the government. In the centre, holding a microphone is Lech Wałęsa (centre)

Extract from a report by Günther Sieber:

Along with the trade unions, strong foundations and a legal counter-revolutionary base are being established in Poland, which may herald the beginning of a softening process. Initially, this process will take the form of pluralism in all the most essential aspects of public life.

At the same time the Polish United Workers Party and its allies have suffered a very heavy defeat in the country. We must take into account that this is the most serious deformation of the socialist system in the Polish People's Republic, so far. The political consequences of the compromises made are assessed as being more far-reaching than those which took place in 1956.

"We will have to somehow put up with the existence of free trade unions, in order not to lose out still further. We know, Comrades, that we have caused you – and particularly you in the German Democratic Republic, although others as well – a great problem. We are also aware of how much political mileage we have supplied to the international labour movement. But for us it is now a question of hours." (Comrade Ryszard Wojna, member of the Central Committee to the Press Attaché on 28th August 1980) [6]

Bogdan Lis:

Once the agreement had been signed, Alina Pienkowska and I immediately found the original and took it out of the Shipyard whilst the celebrations were still going on. We hid it in a private apartment.   [19]

Special communiqué from the Paris Commune Shipyard. Scheduled programme of vacation of the Shipyard:

1. Members of the workforce of the Shipyard to carry out cleaning-up works including the dismantling of objects set up for strike purposes and general tidying-up of the shipyard premises and grounds.

2. Once the cleaning-up process has been finished, the Shipyard will be vacated department by department at 1-hourly intervals, in accordance with the following arrangements. [...]

3. Sentry posts and the Strike Committee will be the last to leave the Shipyard. [...]   [8]

Sławomir Biegański (journalist):

The most difficult work came when the talks were over. A wild horde of my fellow journalists surrounded the presidential table. They made the people in front crouch down so as not to obscure the view of the heroes of the hour. They piled on top of each other. It was incredibly close in the room, my shirt and trousers were dripping wet. And then there was the tension — will I get a picture? Swedes, Germans, Frenchmen, Americans — each one wielding his camera regardless. Each unfortunate move could spell the loss of a good shot. Apart from the

commotion there was also an extraordinary feeling of elation: God, the matter has come to an end and a good end at that...

That day I stayed on the Shipyard premises till late. I don't know what made me go back to the empty conference room. Perhaps I was expecting something unusual? Or was it that I was just sorry to have to leave the place.   [17]

Andrzej Kołodziej:

I was gripped with emotion at the moment of signing the agreement, my throat constricted. But then afterwards, when I left for Gdynia once the strike was over, I felt a sort of emptiness, regret for something lost. The streets were full of workers with rolled blankets under their arms. The nameless heroes of that great strike, where we had won something we would not have thought possible two weeks earlier.   [25]

Józef Częścik (teacher, Gdańsk):

I walked alongside the Shipyard walls. I read the graffiti. This was where people had put in words all that was troubling them. There was a great deal of bitterness. So that's it — I thought — that's how life begins anew: by washing the slate clean.   [20]

Urszula Radek (Świdnik):

In August 1980 I had some unexpected guests staying with me, two young Byelorussians of Polish extraction. Together we watched the signing of the Agreements on television and we all cried with emotion. One of them said despondently: *"When will something like that happen in our country? Surely never!"*.   [20]

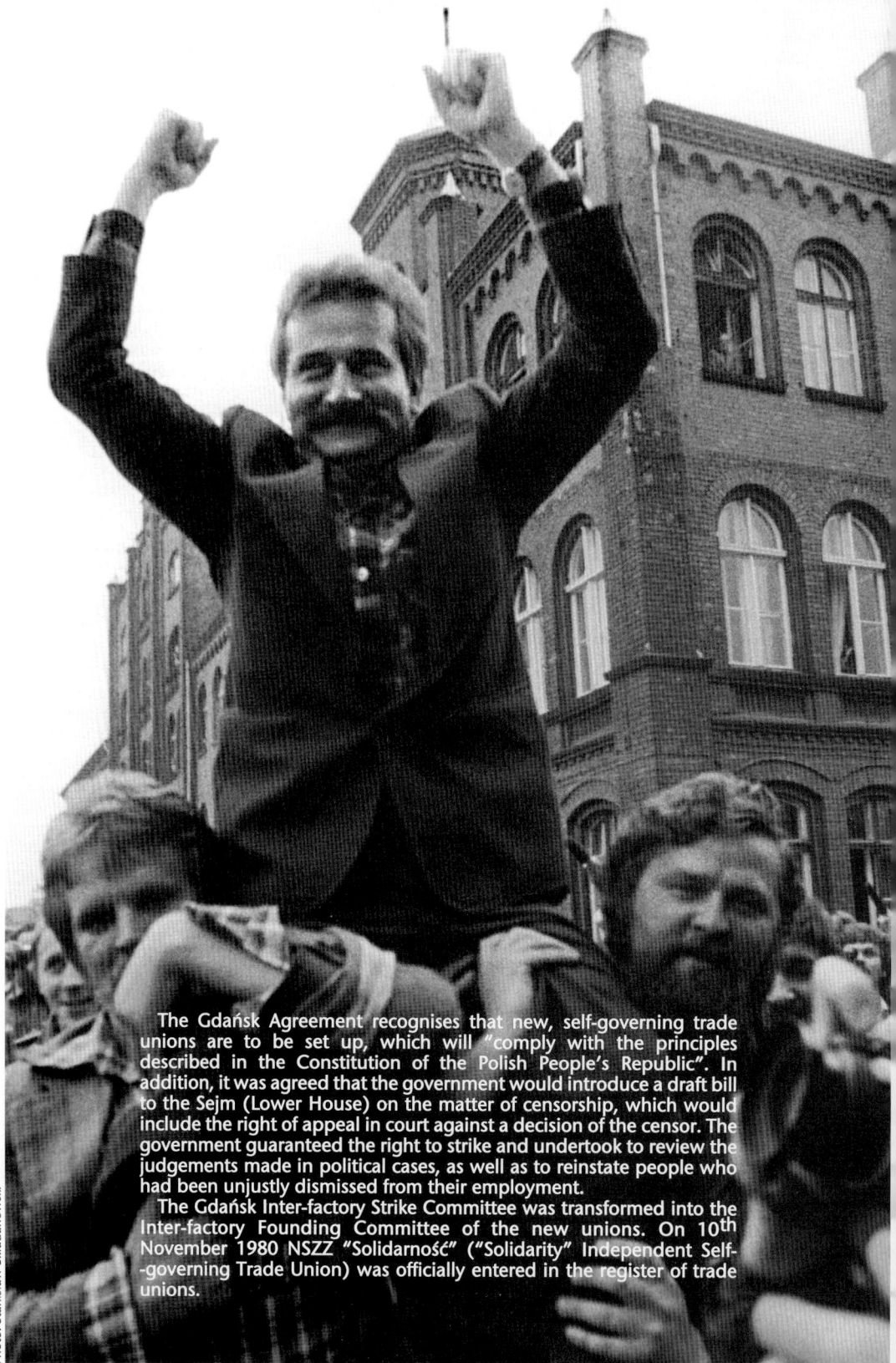

The Gdańsk Agreement recognises that new, self-governing trade unions are to be set up, which will "comply with the principles described in the Constitution of the Polish People's Republic". In addition, it was agreed that the government would introduce a draft bill to the Sejm (Lower House) on the matter of censorship, which would include the right of appeal in court against a decision of the censor. The government guaranteed the right to strike and undertook to review the judgements made in political cases, as well as to reinstate people who had been unjustly dismissed from their employment.

The Gdańsk Inter-factory Strike Committee was transformed into the Inter-factory Founding Committee of the new unions. On 10th November 1980 NSZZ "Solidarność" ("Solidarity" Independent Self-governing Trade Union) was officially entered in the register of trade unions.

Source material used:

Archives:

1. Archiwum Akt Nowych, zespół KC PZPR [Public Records, Department dealing with Central Committee of the Polish United Workers' Party].
2. Archiwum Ministerstwa Spraw Wewnętrznych i Administracji [Archives of the Ministry of Internal Affairs and Administration].
3. Archiwum Państwowe w Gdańsku [State Archives in Gdańsk].
4. Archiwum Urzędu Ochrony Państwa [Archives of the State Security Department].
5. Open Society Archives in Budapest.
6. Archives of the East German Intelligence Service STASI, the so-called Gauck Department of Berlin

Printed sources:

7. "Biuletyn Informacyjny" ["Information Bulletin"], Komitet Obrony Robotników [KOR], Warsaw 1980, no. 6.
8. Zapis wydarzeń. Gdańsk – Sierpień 1980. Dokumenty [Record of Events. Gdańsk – August 1980. Documents], edited by Andrzej Drzycimski, Tadeusz Skutnik, Warsaw 2000.
9. Gdańsk. Sierpień 1980. Rozmowy [Gdańsk. August 1980. Discussions], edited by Andrzej Drzycimski, Tadeusz Skutnik, Gdańsk 1990.
10. Gdańsk. Sierpień 1980. Rozmowy Komisji Rządowej z Międzyzakładowym Komitetem Strajkowym [Gdańsk. August 1980. Discussions between the Government Commission and the Inter-factory Strike Committee], Warsaw 1981.
11. Wojciech Giełżyński, Lech Stefański, Gdańsk. Sierpień 80 [Gdańsk. August 80], Warsaw 1981.
12. Edward Gierek, Przerwana dekada [An Interrupted Decade], Warsaw 1990.
13. Janina Jankowska, Polski Sierpień [Polish August] (a radio report).
14. Jacek Kuroń, Gwiezdny czas. "Wiary i winy" dalszy ciąg [Starry Times. "Beliefs and Faults" contd], London 1991.
15. Moje lato 80 [My Summer of 1980], "Polityka" no. 45, 8.11.1980.
16. "Cold War International History Project Bulletin 11", winter 1998, "In Case Military Assistance Is Provided To Poland", by Mark Kramer.
17. Kto tu wpuścił dziennikarzy? [Who let the Journalists in?], based on a Marek Miller concept, NOWA, Warsaw [1985].
18. PRL w oczach STASI [The Polish People's Republic in the eyes of the STASI], edited by Włodzimierz Borodziej, Jerzy Kochanowski, vol. II, Warsaw 1996.
19. Sierpień 80. Co pozostało z tamtych dni? [August 80. What is left of those days?], ed. Jan Kulas, Gdańsk 1996.
20. Sierpień 80 we wspomnieniach [August 80 in reminiscences], ed. Marek Latoszek, Gdańsk 1991.
21. Sierpień 1980 w Szczecinie. Kalendarium [August 1980 in Szczecin. A Calendar of Events], narratives, Szczecin 1981.
22. Krzysztof Jagielski, Za burtą legendy [Beyond the Legend], Szczecin 1992.
23. Lech Wałęsa, Droga nadziei [The Road of Hope], Kraków 1990.
24. Tajne dokumenty Biura Politycznego. PZPR a "Solidarność" 1980–1981[Secret Documents of the Political Office. PZPR and "Solidarity"], ed. Zbigniew Włodek, London 1992.
25. Alfred Znamierowski, Zaciskanie pięści. Rzecz o Solidarności Walczącej [Clenched Fists. A Tale of Militant Solidarity], Gdynia 1989.
26. Dzień jedności. Bogdan Borusewicz w rozmowie z Jarosławem Kurskim [Day of Unity. Bogdan Borusewicz in conversation with Jarosław Kurski], "Gazeta Wyborcza" 19–20.08.2000.
27. Potrzebna jest wytrwałość. Wywiad z Bogdanem Borusewiczem [Tencity is Essential. An Interview with Bogdan Borusewicz], "Przegląd Polityczny" no. 9/1987.
28. Czułem tę wrogość. Mieczysław Jagielski w rozmowie z Anną Bikont [I Felt the Antipathy. Mieczysław Jagielski in conversation with Anna Bikont], "Gazeta Wyborcza" 30.08.1995.
29. Andrzej Kaczyński, Nasz znak [Our sign], "Tygodnik Solidarność" no. 1, 3.04.1981.
30. Wyniosło mnie w górę. Wspomnienia uczestników Sierpnia 80 [I was borne aloft. Memoirs of participants in August 80], edited by Joanna Szczęsna, Jarosław Kurski, "Gazeta Wyborcza" 29.08.1998.
31. Antoni Rajkiewicz, Ostatni tydzień [The Last Week], "Polityka" no. 35, 1.09.1990.
32. Tomasz Mianowicz, Krok do tyłu [A Step Back], "Rzeczpospolita", 29-30.08.1998.
33. Kazimierz Wójcicki, Rozmowy z księdzem Hilarym Jastakiem [Conversations with Fr. Hilary Jastak], Gdynia 1994, vol. 2.
34. Jerzy Borowczak, Człowiek rodzi się i żyje wolnym [Man is born free and lives free], recorded by K. Wyszkowski, "Tygodnik Solidarność" no. 20, 14.08.1981.
35. Sierpień 1980 roku w Szczecinie. Wydarzenia i dokumenty [August 1980 in Szczecin. Events and Documents], SZSP 1981.
36. Nigdy już nie będę szedł bezbronny z rękami do góry. Rozmowa ze Stanisławem Wądołowskim [I'll never again be unarmed and with my arms in the air. A conversation with Stanisław Wądołowski], M. Kowalski, "Tygodnik Solidarność" no. 21 z 21.08.1981.
37. An Account by Bogdan Borusewicz, recorded by Zbigniew Gluza in 2000 in Warsaw and KARTA Centre Collection (Underground newspapers and publications, official newspapers, leaflets, strike documents, documents relating to the Church, diaries, acco-

The KARTA Centre

A non-governmental organisation providing a service to the public (registered as a Foundation) and dealing with the documentation and popularisation of the contemporary history of Poland and Central & Eastern Europe. It continues the activities of the "Karta" publication, which was set up during martial law in January 1982 and was published clandestinely until the political climate in Poland changed, as well as the activities of the "Eastern Archives" which was set up in 1987 as an organisation independent of the State.

Main undertakings of KARTA:

"Karta" historical quarterly (published officially since 1991, 44 editions to date) – devoted to the social history of Poland and Eastern Europe in the 20th Century. Source material from contemporary witnesses – diaries, memoirs, accounts, letters, documents and copious photographs – enables the publication to show history, above all, from the point of view of the individual. It describes little known or problematical aspects of the past, attempts to break down myths and stereotyping, particularly in relations between the nations. A collection of the "Karta" texts has been published in German (3 volumes) and in Russian (one volume). Special editions devoted to one specific theme have also been prepared by "Karta's" editorial team: *Dni Solidarności* [*The Days of Solidarity*] in English, Spanish, German and Ukrainian and *Koniec Jałty* [*The End of Yalta*] in English and Spanish.

The KARTA Publishing House produces books dealing with the history of the 20th Century, as well as series of publications, such as: "Polish Jews" (Polish-language documentation of the Holocaust), "A Biographical Dictionary of Dissidents in the Polish People's Republic", "Poland- Ukraine: Difficult Questions" (a Polish-Ukrainian dialogue concerned with the WW2 period), and "Index of the Repressed".

Index of the Repressed – a programme which has been on-going since 1988, documenting the fate of named individuals who were victims of repression in the USSR after 17th September 1939 (computerised data-base contains approx. 750 records), as well as the victims of the Ukrainian-Polish conflict of 1942–1947 (25,000 records). Lists of names, verified within individual categories of repression, are published in subsequent volumes (approx. 120,000 biographical entries) and are also available on the internet. For the last three years, this programme has been run under the auspices of the Institute of National Remembrance.

Centre's Archives – these document the 20th Century "social" history of Poland and her immediate neighbours and, in particular, those subjects which have either not been documented at all or only superficially. The Centre is especially concerned with the collecting of personal records (memoirs, diaries, accounts) of individual people who have been witness to history in the making. The Centre's archives (some 1300 running metres) include, among others:

Eastern Archives – deal with the fate of Polish citizens on the Eastern borderlands of the II Polish Republic and the USSR (1917–56), it collects accounts and documents from private individuals, witness accounts, and also carries out research in the archives of the countries of the former USSR.

Opposition Archives – collects material from the period 1944–89, mostly concerning the opposition to the Communist authorities, starting with the armed underground during the Stalinist era, through to subsequent political changes, the activities of the democratic opposition and "Solidarity". The largest collection comprises underground publications and books, published beyond the censor's reach, during the period 1976–89. The "Solidarity – the birth of a movement" Collection (dating from the years 1980–81) has been entered on the UNESCO World Heritage List's "Memory of the World" programme.

Photograph Archives – collects photographs of a social history nature from the period 1890–1990; it holds over 110,000 photographs and includes several individual photographers' compilations as well as several dozen thematic collections.

Oral History Archives – comprises almost 2000 oral accounts, recorded during the